ALL OUR CHILDREN

A WINDOW ON THE WORLD OF CHILDHOOD

JUDITH AND MARTIN WOODHEAD

RINGPRESS

ACKNOWLEDGEMENTS

We would like to thank warmly all those who helped us write this book, especially:

David Brown, Series Producer of All Our Children, who gave support and advice in countless ways over several years;

Edward Barnes, John Percival, Howard Reid and **Renny Rye**, who produced the film sequences on which the chapters are based, and **June Robinson**, their researcher who kindly assisted us;

The **cameramen** and **assistants**, **sound recordists**, **electricians**, **film editors**, **production assistants** and **location researchers**, who provided photographs of the children;

Geoff Stimson at Ringpress, who designed the book and edited the manuscript;

The **children** themselves, who willingly shared their stories and increased our respect for their world of childhood.

RINGPRESS

An imprint of Ringpress Ltd.
Spirella House, Letchworth, Hertfordshire SG6 4ET

Text © Judith and Martin Woodhead and Ringpress Books 1990

First published 1990

ISBN No: 0948955 01 5

Typeset by Ringpress Books
Production consultants: Landmark Ltd.
Printed and bound in Spain by Graficas Estella SA

CONTENTS

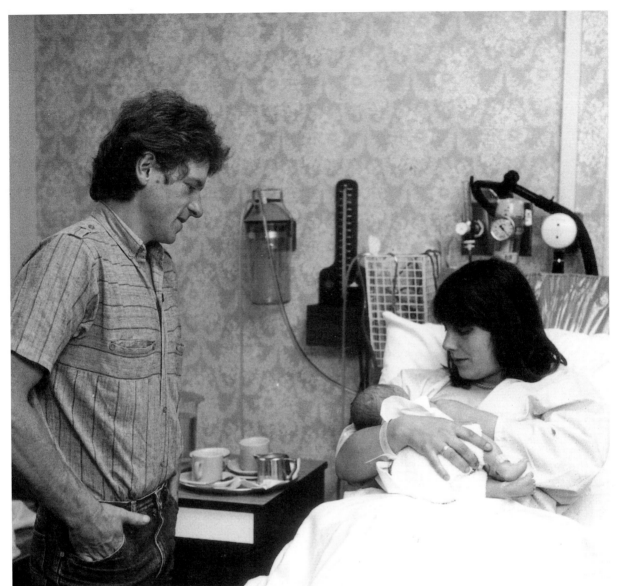

SMALL BEGINNING: *Fiona holds Jenny as Jonty looks on...and All Our Children is born.*

INTRODUCTION

"HAVE you got a name for a girl?" asked the midwife.

"Jenny." There was no hesitation in Fiona's voice as she named her daughter, just powerful feelings of relief and joy for a new life, and a fourth member of her young family.

It was 4.30 in the morning on May 19, 1987. Fiona had walked into the labour room in Yorkshire, England only seven and a half minutes earlier. And now already here was a new baby, Jenny, cradled in her arms. Through the hospital windows, the horizon was just beginning to glow crimson at the dawn of Jenny's first day.

There was nothing exceptional about Jenny's birth, except in one important respect, the presence of a BBC television crew. Filming the first few moments of Jenny's life was the beginning of a major documentary series all about the world of childhood. This is the book of that series. It documents the lives of more than fifty of the children featured in twelve television programmes. But these are not just the forgettable myriad of 'other people's children', unnamed millions for whom we feel a vague sense of shared responsibility. These are real children, each with an individual personality, with a story to tell and feelings to share. They are ALL OUR CHILDREN.

Jenny is one of about 350,000 babies born all over the world on that day. The BBC filmed five more births during the summer of 1987, in locations as far apart as the inner suburbs of Budapest, a village in southern India, a textile town in central China, a favela in Rio de Janeiro, and a rural settlement in Kenya. For the next two and a half years all six babies were regularly filmed as they got to know their brothers and sisters, learned to walk, talk and feed themselves, and began to explore the different worlds into which they had been born. But the stories of these six babies are only the beginning.

ALL OUR CHILDREN is about childhood at every age, from birth right through to adolescence. Many of the children bear the scars of suffering – victims of poverty, ignorance and exploitation. But not all. We challenge the conventional image of children as passive and helpless in the fight for a better life. There are children out there in the front line, campaigning for a decent standard of health for all children. We meet other children who have a more personal battle to fight, to find their way through childhood with a physical or mental disability. What awareness do they have of their situation? How do they cope with it?

ALL OUR CHILDREN presents the world of childhood through children's eyes. It is the children themselves who tell their stories. They speak directly to us, in their own way and in their own words. And frequently it is the least worldly and educated who speak with most confidence and eloquence. A Quechan Indian girl in Ecuador explains that she is a Catholic, but she also believes in praying to the mountain god for rain. Does she recognise anything strange about her combination of beliefs? An eleven-year-old Sri Lankan boy has already taken the vows to remain a Buddhist monk for the rest of his life. Does he have any regrets about giving up his childhood so soon?

ALL OUR CHILDREN shows that there is no such thing as a normal childhood. We meet a boy whose home is nothing more than a makeshift tent on an Indian building site, a girl in an orphanage in Brazil, an American boy who has been through divorce...twice, a girl growing up in a travelling family in Eire, a refugee child from the war in Mozambique. What does each of these children think about what home is, or was, or should be?

Many of the children are developing their potential as mathematicians and linguists, musicians and dancers, acrobats and footballers. Different societies value different skills, but what does it mean to these children to become so accomplished? Are they missing out on anything?

ALL OUR CHILDREN also looks at aspects that unite children the world over, such as their love of play. Modern children are bombarded with toys and playthings, from their first rattle to the latest electronically-controlled robot. Do they really gain from all the expense and clutter? Other children use their imaginations to create something out of nothing.

Perhaps the most common feature of childhood is the near-universal requirement that all children go to school. All over the world classrooms look the same. The competitive scramble for achievement is a mixed blessing, with few success stories and many more failures. What does it feel like to go to school for the first time? What is it like to go to a school that challenges tradition?

Of course the ALL OUR CHILDREN team could not ask the six babies for an interview. So we turned to the next best thing, the babies' older sisters and brothers who are growing up alongside them. But even tiny babies do not stay helpless for long. By the time the last filming was complete and the book was finished, Jenny was already chattering to her mother and helping to change her new-born brother's nappy. She is already beginning to understand how to take care of a little one even younger and more helpless than herself. Sometimes they squabble and sometimes they fight, but children also care for other children all over the world.

For every baby born into the world, another child is about to leave childhood behind. So ALL OUR CHILDREN returns to the communities where our six babies were born to meet girls and boys around twelve years old who are moving into adolescence. What are their problems and their hopes? How do they see the worlds that they have grown up in, both looking back and looking forwards?

Making children themselves the focus of ALL OUR CHILDREN led to some surprises. We all think we know what it means to be a child. We have all been children and most of us have children of our own. But children do not always see their world the way adults do. They constantly surprise and baffle us. For adults, the image of children playing in a disease-infested gutter, or toiling long hours on a sugar plantation, provokes a sense of moral outrage and condemnation of the continuing abuse of children's vulnerability. But ask the children about their situation and you are just as likely to get a big grin as a look of despair.

ALL OUR CHILDREN is a reminder that children do not condemn the quality of their lives as readily as adults might. To do so would be to condemn themselves. To be a shoeshine boy or

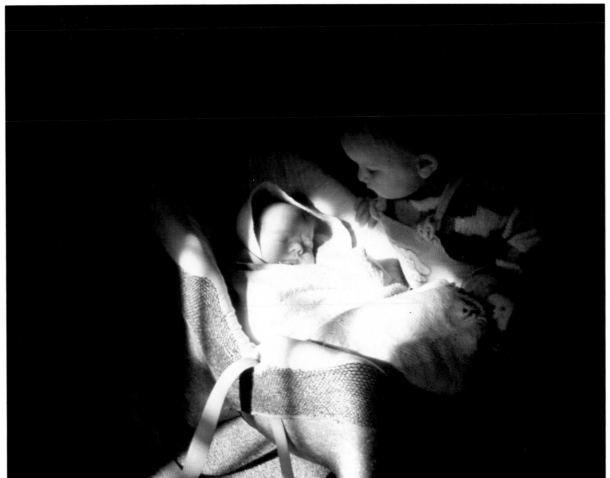

FULL CIRCLE: Now Jenny is the big one, who starts learning to live with baby brother Josh.

a garbage sorter is their life, the only one they know, and very often the only prospect they can imagine. They rarely complain. They are too busy getting on with living, learning, and playing whenever they get the chance. And their faces often tell the same story. Some do look pale, weary and apathetic, but many others are bright-eyed, full of jokes and laughter. Such children seem capable of smiling through almost any adversity. Their good humour does not justify our complacency, but it does give pause for thought.

ALL OUR CHILDREN is certainly a record of children's continuing vulnerability in the modern world. But it is also a tribute to their immense resilience and their great sense of fun.

JUDITH AND MARTIN WOODHEAD

CHAPTER ONE: NEW LIVES

JENNY: FIRST IMPRESSIONS

'She didn't like her new baby brother at first. She said: I'm still the baby. She's funny when she's cross. She stamps her foot and falls over'

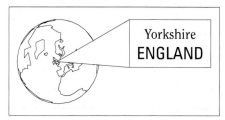

Yorkshire
ENGLAND

AT A TINY cottage in a North Yorkshire dale three excited children woke up to find their granny in the house, their mother and father missing and some special news. They had a new sister called Jenny. Amy for one was glad that she was no longer the only girl: "I wanted it to be a girl and Simeon and Daddy wanted it to be a boy," she said. "But then Simeon changed his mind and wanted to call it Cherry Cake."

The Turner family live in a small rented cottage on the village green in one of Britain's smallest farming communities. Jonty works as a general farm labourer, and occasional construction worker. It is not an easy way to make a living. They have no chance of buying their own place and they are frequently strapped for cash, but it is where they want to live and bring up their children. Jonty was born in the village and went to the same one-room school where his eldest children are now taught. He went away to college for a while, but soon came back. Fiona is also Yorkshire-born. She had never heard of the village until she took on a job at the local hotel soon after completing her training as a nursery nurse. She had no plans to stay beyond the summer, but meeting Jonty at the village pub soon changed that. They married and settled down to raise a family.

Back at the cottage, that family was now looking forward to meeting the new arrival for the first time. Later that day, Jonty started out on his third drive down the dale in twelve hours, taking Amy and Simeon to visit their mum and baby Jenny in hospital. He was just a little bit weary, but Amy was not going to make any allowances for that. She was full of chat and questions. As they drove, Simeon was sleepy and more than usually quiet, but once inside the hospital, he woke and ran ahead to find his mother's bed. "Mum, I haven't seen you for a long, long time," he said. When you're three, a few hours can seem to be forever. Beaming down proudly into his tiny sister's crib, Simeon thought he saw a likeness. "She looks like me!" he said proudly.

"I hope not," joked Jonty. "We don't want another like you."

Simeon had never been into a hospital before and he was desperate to find out how all the knobs and levers could be used to make his mother's bed go up and down. Fiona had been wondering how the children would get on with Jenny when they were all back home together. "I think Amy will thoroughly enjoy having another baby," she said. "She'll mother her. In fact she'll probably want to mother her too much. I don't know about the boys. Simeon will probably ignore her as much as possible, and Edward – I don't think he's going to like her very much, probably because of the attention I'll have to give her – but he'll get used to it."

Soon it was time for Jonty to take the children back home. He had been watching Jenny curled

WAITING: Jonty, Fiona, Amy, Edward and Simeon before the arrival of new baby Jenny.

up peacefully in her crib. It seemed like a good omen. "Is she still asleep through all this racket?" he asked. "She'll be all right at our house then!"

Jenny settled into daily life at the cottage more easily than Fiona could have imagined. She fed well, slept well, and did not seem to suffer too badly with colic. Fiona's friends flattered her by saying that she was an expert mum fourth time around. But Fiona suspected it was because she had too many other demands on her time to notice any minor irritations. Certainly Jenny was a very easy-going baby, happy to be cuddled and carried by the big ones. More than anything else she was a very watchful child. As soon as she could lift her head and focus she seemed to be quietly absorbing everything around her. And with three older children around the house she had plenty to take in.

Fiona and Jonty have a very easy-going approach to bringing up children. "After all," they joke, "we've little choice. We're outnumbered two-to-one."

There is an absolute minimum of rules and discipline. For the most part they let the children get on with it, setting up their toys in whatever room they fancy. Not that they always play happily together, far from it. Squabbles are inevitable and frequent, especially with fiery tempers like Simeon's about. But Fiona never interferes unless things are getting out of hand.

In summer, the dale is a delightful place to grow up in. On warm afternoons, baby Jenny could be wheeled out in her traditional high-sprung pram across the field and down to the fast-flowing river for a picnic and a paddle. For Simeon that usually meant a complete soaking.

But once the long winter began, it was a different story. Jenny's horizon was confined to the

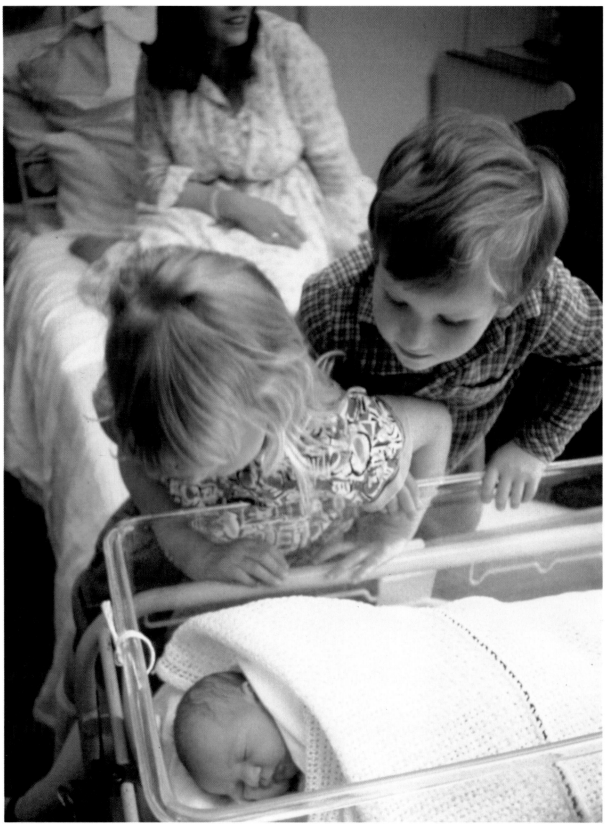

NEW SISTER: 'Amy will mother the new baby, but Simeon will ignore her,' says Fiona.

BIG SISTER: 'When Josh came home, Jenny thought that she was still the youngest.'

four walls of the cottage, except when she was tucked snugly under Fiona's sheepskin coat to take Amy to school, or when she was strapped into the car for the weekly supermarket trip to the nearest town. During Jenny's first winter, the family spent most of their time in the sitting room. It was the only warm room in the house, with a well-banked coal fire working overtime against the draughts, especially when a wet north-easterly wind was blowing down the dale. Not that the children seemed to notice the cold.

Jenny's first winter was long and sometimes trying with more than a fair share of coughs and colds. Fiona found the television and video a blessing. They were on a lot of the day, with Jenny soon discovering children's programmes such as *Playbus* and *Rainbow*, not to forget the local hero *Postman Pat* and a lot else besides.

One Sunday evening, shortly after Jenny's first Christmas, the children were sitting by the fire watching *The Lion, The Witch And The Wardrobe*. Jenny soon lost interest, finding it much more fun to shake pine needles off the lowest branches of the Christmas tree. In the process she sent a Father Christmas candle smashing to the floor. Without another thought, Fiona gathered up the broken pieces, pulled back the fireguard and threw them into the hearth. The effect was immediate, spectacular and just a little alarming. The fire was fuelled into a roar by the burning paraffin wax, sending flames shooting up the chimney. Jonty took one look and went outside into the cold night air. He returned immediately, looked at Fiona and, with a voice as controlled as the captain of a sinking ship, asked: "What do you do if your chimney's on fire?"

Twenty minutes later the children were roused from *The Lion, The Witch And The Wardrobe*, by Fiona whispering quietly: "Children! Go and look out of the window!"

Amy, Simeon, Edward and Jenny could barely believe what they saw. "Is Fireman Sam coming in?" asked Edward in wide-eyed disbelief.

Soon the sitting room was full of black-booted firemen, shovelling out the fire and later drinking mugs of tea as a reward for their trouble. Throughout Jenny sat in the middle of the easy chair and watched, taking it all in.

Jenny's first birthday was a grand event for everyone. Amy remembers the party. "Me, Katie, Emma, Simeon and Edward opened the presents and we just threw the paper all over. So Jenny just crawled around and played with it. And then we had tea. First, mummy lit the candle and mummy and Jenny blew it out. Then we had a few games while Jenny was in the kitchen with Edward, and then the birthday cake was cut. There was sort of a Daddy bear, a Mummy bear and a baby bear."

While she was tiny, Jenny had slept in a carry-cot on her mother's dressing table. Later she was transferred to a cot at the foot of her parents' bed. But by her first birthday, they decided she was old enough to move into Amy's bedroom. Amy soon became a second mother to her sister, just as Fiona had predicted. "Amy's become particularly helpful since Jenny's been big enough to make her demands known. She'll get her out of bed in the morning and play with her before anybody else is up. We've often got up at 7 o' clock in the morning and found Amy's already given Jenny her breakfast, changed her and dressed her. Sometimes we've wondered whether we put too much on Amy, but really she puts it on herself."

Amy seemed to love every minute of it, especially when her little sister let her boss her around: "I ask her to 'come here' and she comes . And I ask her to help tidy up and she does it. Like she puts her Lego away or opens a bag for me to put toys in. And she can help mummy, too. She tries to sweep the floor and she gives mummy things when she wants them, things like pieces of coal that have fallen out of the fire and things like little beads from the floor. And polishing – she just gets the cloth and rubs it on everything."

Once Jenny started to talk and play with the others, her position as the fourth and final child in the family seemed secure. Jonty thought he had made sure of that. But then quite out of the blue, came a bombshell. Jonty explains: "We were told over the telephone. The specialist thought it was great – the first repeat vasectomy he's ever had to do in 21 years. But for us it was a great shock, it certainly was. We'd already decided that we weren't going to have any more children. It didn't seem fair to the others in terms of giving them attention – I mean there are only so many hours in the day. And I suppose from a purely selfish point of view I was glad to see Jenny progressing out of the most demanding stage. Like once she began to sleep all through the night I thought: 'Great, that's no more disturbed nights. And the next thing will be when there's no more nappies and all that carry-on.' Now we're starting it all over again."

Fiona was expecting her fifth baby. It was a worry to them how they would cope, not least financially. Jonty had never earned much on the farm, and now much of that work had dried up. More and more he was relying on what he could earn from working for a builder friend, which was not much. There was no way they wanted to uproot the family and move in search of better prospects in a bigger town, such as Skipton or Keighley. In desperation, Jonty even took a job on a North Sea oil rig, working away from home for two weeks at a time and then having two weeks off. It was hard, but at least they could pay the bills. But things did not work out and Jonty was laid off in the aftermath of the Piper Alpha disaster. He came back to working in the dale and life returned to normal.

A few months before Jenny's second birthday, he found himself once again driving the oldest children to the hospital to meet their newborn, a boy called Josh. This time Edward was old enough to go too, but he was struggling to understand quite where this latest member of the family fitted in. Fiona did her best to explain: "He's your little brother."

"And yours," said Edward.

Fiona tried again: "He's not my little brother."

After a long pause, Edward offered a compromise: "He's everybody's likkle bruvver."

Jenny knew nothing of all this. She had been to stay with her grandpa who had recently come to live nearby. Her first encounter with Josh came later when grandpa brought her back home and told her to go and find mum. She climbed up the stairs to her parents' bedroom to find Fiona sitting on the bed, just finishing feeding Josh. She approached cautiously, quiet and watchful as ever, and gazed intently at the tiny being who had displaced her in her mother's arms. Fiona picked her up to show that there was easily room for both of them on her lap. Jenny began to explore, gingerly at first, but gaining confidence, touching Josh's tiny feet, his fingers, and his face. It took quite a while for Jenny to get used to the idea as Amy remembered later: "When Josh came home, Jenny thought that she was still the youngest. She thought that it wasn't a baby belonging to her family. She thought she was still the baby. She got cross and said things like: 'I'm still the baby.' She's funny when she's cross. She stamps her foot and falls over. But she still likes to hold him a lot and play with him now, with teddies and rattles and tickling him."

MARIANNA: SURPRISE BABY

'Yes, she's always sick and giving us too much expense on medicines. But she didn't ask to come into the world and she's the thing we love most in life'

Rio
BRAZIL

FIVE children was enough, decided Sueli and her husband Fernando, living high on a crowded hillside above Rio de Janeiro. Sueli would be sterilised. But when she went to the doctor, she was in for a surprise.

Sueli remembers: "He said: 'I can't do the operation.' I said: 'Why not?' He said: 'Because you're pregnant'."

A bad start to a difficult pregnancy, with dates unclear, and followed by a nightmare of a birth, at least six weeks premature, and a desperate battle in an incubator. For baby Marianna, life had got off to an unpromising beginning.

Marianna's family live above Rio in the crowded Santa Marta favela. It is home for more than 10,000 people and their shack is right at the top. They like it up there despite the daily 300-step climb. It is quieter at the top and there is a bit more space for the children to play. They call their tiny makeshift home No 1 Tranquillity Street. Not that there is much tranquillity in Marianna's life. She is the sixth in line, with one big brother, Luis Fernando who is 15, and four sisters Fabiana, 12, Christiana, 9, Luciana, 7, and Marie Fernanda, 3.

Fernando and Sueli would not live anywhere else. They like Rio. It is an exciting city, not just at carnival time. The schools and creches are better than in the provinces and there are good hospitals backed by a government aid programme. Even so, the cost of living is high and they can only earn enough to live on by working long hours in low-paid jobs down in Rio. Fernando works in a plant shop on the sea front and Sueli is a housemaid. Very often she cannot get home until after her youngest children are in bed. But Sueli is a tough woman with enormous stamina.

Fabiana recalls Marianna's birth. "My mother felt her first pains at work but they were only weak, so she went to where my father works. They went shopping, then came home. She put the groceries away and made the evening meal, gave my sisters a bath and put them to bed. Then she started to feel a stronger pain, so my father took her down to the clinic."

Then Sueli's longest night began.

"It was terrible," she says. "It was half past ten at night. I'd been haemorrhaging, but I knew it was too early. The doctor examined me and then said: 'Look, madam, there's no room for you here.' I waited another fifteen minutes, and then he examined me again. He said that I was putting on an act and that the baby wasn't due yet. I told him: 'Doctor, I'm the mother of five children. I know very well what it feels like when a woman is about to have a baby.'

"The pain was unbearable and I was afraid my baby might be born any minute. But the doctor just kept saying he couldn't do anything about it because he had no spare beds. Then my husband started arguing with the security men, saying that I was going to have the baby right there at the entrance to the clinic. But I left and my husband followed.

"We caught a bus to the big maternity hospital down by the ferry station, right across the other side of Rio. It was half past one at night. The people there were really nice. They put me on a drip to hold her back. But it wasn't any use and by the middle of the next day they took the drip away. After that it was a five-minute affair. There was just one pain and she was born. She was the only one of my babies that didn't give me a hard time.

"The treatment at the hospital was excellent and the doctors and nurses were very good. They treated me very well, although it was free of charge. It was very good, the best."

Fernando was not allowed to attend the birth, so the first he saw of his new daughter was later that day – a three-pound pink bundle, bandaged up with tubes, electrodes and ventilators inside a brightly-lit incubator.

The doctor said her chances were good, but Fernando is a gentle-hearted man and could not conceal his emotions, not even from seven-year-old Luciana. She remembers the next time she saw him. "When my father came home he was crying because Marianna was in an incubator."

By the time Fernando went back to visit Sueli next day, she was already able to report an improvement.

"They took an X-ray to see if her little lungs are still weak," she told him. "She's on a drip and she's still on oxygen. But yesterday we started giving her milk – five lots of milk and the

HARD CLIMB: 'She has given me a new life.'

paediatrician says she's already put on 100 grammes. I am as happy as anything. She's really clever." The oxygen was removed soon afterwards and Marianna began to put on weight steadily. Even so, the doctors did not expect her to catch up until she was at least 5-6 months old.

The children were disappointed when their mother returned home three days later without the baby. For the next month she went back to the hospital every day to express breast milk and to hold and cuddle Marianna.

"We were very worried," says Fabiana. "Whenever my mother came home she used to bring us news of her. We prayed for her. And whenever she got very bad we felt sad. Me and my sisters, we all cried, cos we felt so sorry for her."

At last, Marianna was allowed home. Sueli carried her triumphantly up the 300 steps, through the squalid poverty of the hot and noisy favela, to a boisterous welcome from the children on Tranquillity Street. Marianna would be carried up those steps many times. The favela is no place for pushchairs, prams or buggies. Babies must be carried everywhere – in arms, on hips, on backs. Once they are crawling, letting infants out of the house is a risky business, with steep falls around every corner. Small boys kick balls around on flat rooftops, tackling each other right up against the edge. Babies get plenty of practice at climbing here, at first on all fours a step at a time, then sliding on their bottoms, until they are eventually bold enough to walk up and down on their own. Once she gets to be a schoolgirl, Marianna can practise her tables on them every day, skipping up and down two or three at a time, backwards and forwards to school, shops or friends' houses.

But coming back home from hospital was not the end of Marianna's difficulties. The first problem was that during the months in hospital Sueli's milk had all but dried up, even though she had offered herself to other mothers in the favela who needed a wet-nurse. Now it was Sueli's turn to call on the community for support.

Luciana explains: "When my mother brought Marianna home, she didn't have any milk in her breasts, so she sent me to get a friend who also has a baby and she fed Marianna. Then she put her to bed and went home. But soon after Marianna started to cry cos she wanted more, so I had to fetch my mother's friend back to feed her again. Later, my mother bought a dummy at the shop and gave it to Marianna."

The demands of looking after Marianna were so intensive during the early months that Sueli made no attempt to go back to work and instead earned a little cash by making sweets to sell around the favela. Then, when Marianna was five months old, she very nearly died of pneumonia. She had already suffered one bout during her first weeks in the maternity hospital and now she was back in hospital again with Sueli spending most of her time going backwards and forwards.

"We've had a lot of costs and we're still having them with antibiotics, doctors' fees and special diets. She's always getting sick and has to stay in the hospital every other month. I have to be with her for five, six or ten days at a time, spending money on the medicines. Yes, she's giving us too much expense, but she didn't ask to come into this world."

As soon as Marianna was well enough, she started having weekly physiotherapy. The therapist was worried about the lack of bodytone and the stiffness in some of her muscles. Luciana remembers those days: "Marianna had to do some exercises so she could walk. First she played with some toys. Then the woman took Marianna's arms and legs. But she started to cry, so my mother had to change her nappy before they could start the exercise again. The woman said she would never be able to walk, but now she's started to walk already." Even so, Marianna was still being carried around on her first birthday, more like an infant than a toddler.

"She really is different from the other children," said Sueli. "She only started to move her hands and her body fully at 8 months. At 9 months she still couldn't sit properly. Now, after one year she's beginning to crawl and get up by herself. She speaks some words, but they're not so clear, and her sense of touch hasn't developed. She can't hold things properly."

All through Marianna's first year, Sueli had been keen to be sterilised at last to make sure that there would be no more babies. But it was not easy to arrange. She could not expect Fernando to stay at home with Marianna because he had just managed to get a better-paid job. Nor did she feel confident about leaving Marianna in Fabiana's care during the several days that she would need to be in hospital. When she did finally manage to get things organised she could not believe what the doctors told her. She was several months pregnant. She had left it too late again.

"Now I'm expecting another baby I don't know what I'm going to do. I'll have to take care of two little babies. I don't know how I'll manage things because we need to take care of Marianna as we would a little baby."

Sueli's seventh child, a girl called Angelica, was born without complications. Within a few months the older sisters had already begun to notice how much more sensitive and delicate Marianna was compared with her younger sister.

"Marianna cries more," said Fabiana. "Angelica only cries when she wants my mother's breast or the bottle. Then she goes back to sleep. But after Marianna's had her bottle she doesn't go to sleep. She wants to have lunch again."

After the shock of Angelica's birth, there was no way the family were going to risk making the same mistake yet again. Fortunately Fernando was able to arrange for his wife to have the operation through a relative of his employer who is a doctor at the hospital.

"I wouldn't have had enough money to pay for the operation myself," he said. "It's very expensive in a private clinic and I don't have that kind of money. We might have had an eighth child, and another, and another, but as things have turned out there won't be any more babies."

Not that Sueli and Fernando resent having such a large family. They are as devoted to their children as they are to each other, which is not true of all their neighbours in the favela. But Marianna is still a puzzle and a problem to them.

"I've had a premature baby before. Christiana was born at 7 months 10 days, but she never gave me as much work as Marianna has. Marianna has respiratory and feeding problems. Sometimes after she gets her milk she spews it out. She has had pneumonia, intestinal infection, chicken pox, measles and German measles. She has had pneumonia three times. Her last disease was a sort of infection of the skin. And when she catches cold she can't breathe properly, so we have to get up to her time after time during the night. I notice the difference between Marianna and Angelica still, though Marianna is getting much better now. Angelica tried to stand on her feet and was almost walking when she was ten months old. Marianna only started walking when she was two.

"Marianna was anaemic and used to fall over a lot, but the doctor gave her some medicine and

COMPETITION: 'When I hold Angelica in my arms, Marianna wants me to hold her too.'

she got better, much better. She stopped falling and started eating. She didn't used to eat properly. Then the doctor gave her a special diet of rice bran, corn bran, toasted manioc leaf and crushed egg shell. I gave it to her and I think she started developing very much better after this.

"Marianna can be very naughty. She throws pebbles at everyone, picks on the neighbours and teases all the children. In the kitchen, she fiddles with the stove. She is jealous of Angelica and attacks her. They fight a lot. When I hold Angelica in my arms, Marianna wants me to hold her too, so I have to hold the two of them. When their dad arrives, they want him to hold them together, too.

"Marianna has taken a lot of looking after. She's so very complicated. But I love her. She has given me a new life. To her father she seems like a first baby. He is overjoyed with her, and the children are really loving and affectionate with her. It takes a lot of doing, but she's the thing that we love the most in life."

JIN JIN: THE ONE AND ONLY

'She seems to think only of herself and it isn't good for her. She's too solitary, too selfish. I hope playing with other children will make her more tolerant'

Xi'an
CHINA

JIN JIN will never know what it is like to have sisters and brothers, nor will any of her friends. She is part of a generation of children born under China's strict one-child policy. Not that she will ever be lonely. She is the constant focus of attention from parents, grandparents, aunts and uncles.

She was born in the maternity clinic at Number 5 Cotton Factory in the central Chinese city of Xi'an, once the historic capital and now a major textile centre. Her mother, Jou Lan, is a supervisor there. She is known as a conscientious worker, a good timekeeper who never once asked for any days off during her pregnancy.

Like her mother, sister and many other relatives, Jou Lan is a member of the huge cotton commune, set at the bottom of a gently-sloping

SINGLE JIN: All her age group are only-children. It's hard.'

hillside just outside the town centre. There are five drab, grey, concrete factories in a line along a wide busy road. They dominate the landscape as well as the lives of the 13,000 workers and their families, most of whom live in the six-storey blocks of flats next to them.

But Jou Lan's family live in one of the few remaining areas that have not been modernised, mostly single storey dwellings of various sizes, laid out on a grid of narrow paths, with occasional courtyards and plenty of mature trees. Jou Lan's home fronts on to one of these courtyards. It is her parents' house where she was brought up with her two younger sisters. They all still live there, along with her husband, Jian Kou, who works as a motor mechanic. They had been married for a year when the baby was due. The family could not agree whether their only child should be a girl or a boy, although Jou Lan secretly longed for "a bouncy little girl". Her wish was granted. Once Jou Lan's pregnancy reached eight months she was given a check-up every week by the factory doctor. That is a rule of the commune. It was during one of those check-ups that her labour began and the doctor accompanied her on the two minute walk across the compound to the clinic along with her husband and mother.

After a long night of waiting, Jin Jin was born in a typical pink-grey Xi'an dawn. Within minutes of the birth the midwife recorded the baby's fingerprints in red ink alongside her mother's. This is not thought of as sinister. It is the first entry on a Baby Development Record Book, which will be updated throughout her childhood. Then she carefully wrapped up the baby in the traditional brightly-coloured swaddling shawl to be held in turn by mother, father and grandmother.

Jou Lan spent a week at the clinic and then left, but not for home. First she and the baby followed another Chinese custom by staying for a month at her father-in-law's house. By tradition he named the baby at a party for all their relatives and friends. He performed the Chinese 'red box ceremony', announcing her as Jin Jin, which means tranquillity.

Finally back at home, Jou Lan could settle down with her new baby.

"I made lots of clothes for Jin Jin," she says. "I knitted socks and hats for her. But I didn't know how to make the cotton padded clothes and quilts that she needs for the winter. So my mother helped me with them."

Jou Lan was entitled to three months maternity leave on full pay. But after that she was expected to return to her full time job. Many mothers put their children into the factory creches but this was not necessary in Jou Lan's case. Her mother had recently given up work and was only too pleased to take care of the baby. Jou Lan did not like leaving Jin Jin every day and the breaks allowed for breastfeeding were not much comfort.

"I work an eight-hour shift, six days a week. The factory makes arrangements for workers who are breastfeeding to have two breaks. One is fifty minutes, the other a hundred minutes, including a mealbreak. It's a ten minute walk to my home so I don't get much time with her. But I want to go on breastfeeding until she's one. Really I'm fortunate because this rule applies only to workers who live in the factory compound. If I lived in the city I wouldn't be allowed to go home because the journey is too long. My baby would have to be fed on cow's milk.

"I can still remember the day Jin Jin took her first step. At that time she was still very unsteady on her feet. There's a saying among old people in China that this is because there's a stone tied to her feet that's pulling her back. If you cut away the stone with a chopper then she can start walking. That's what my mother did to help Jin Jin. Not literally! She banged on the floor behind her heels, as if to chop away the stone. At the same time I squatted down in front of Jin Jin and encouraged her to walk towards me, step by step. It worked!"

Then Jin Jin's father left his job in the state-run garage and set up his own business. Under recent government reforms he had applied for a Private Enterprise Licence and borrowed 40,000 Yuen to establish the 'Jian Kou Garage' with eight employees. At the same time he had grown frustrated by bringing up Jin Jin at his in-laws' house, and the three of them moved to a first-floor apartment of a farmhouse a little way off. Jou Lan had never lived away from her parents' house before and she was not happy with the new arrangement. Jou Lan says: "Jin Jin doesn't

SPLIT: Jin Jin missed her father. She used to sleep with him while mum was on night shift.

seem to like it much because it's all strange and she doesn't know her way around. She still prefers her grandmother's house. And it's not convenient for me either. Of course it means I can be more independent, but it's too far away from my work."

Day after day they were alone together in the apartment without the support of their family, while Jian Kou was spending longer and longer trying to make his new venture work. Jou Lan was not happy. Eventually she decided to take her baby back to her parents' house. Meanwhile Jian Kou's business failed and he went back at his old job as a mechanic. The family have seen very little of him since.

By the age of one, Jin Jin was the only child of a single-parent family. She missed her father, especially at night, because she used to sleep alongside him more often than her mother, who was often on the night shift.

By now Jin Jin was starting to talk. "The first word she said was 'aunty', then 'daddy', 'mummy', 'grandma' and so on," said Jou Lan. "She said 'aunty' first because of my younger sister, who works in the factory. Sometimes on her way home she buys sweets. So Jin Jin likes her aunty very much. She rummages through her pockets to see if she has brought something back for her. Now when I take her out she sees ice-cream or lollies and calls out: 'Buy, buy'. Sometimes when grandad comes home she says: 'Grandad money' because she wants him to buy her something. Everyone spoils her. When she is outside all the neighbours and the big children pick her up and make a fuss of her. She always wants someone to pick her up.

"Jin Jin is an only child. It was different for me. I grew up with two sisters, both younger than me. When the three of us were together, I obviously had to look after my younger sisters, and whenever I did anything I had to think of them. But Jin Jin seems to think only of herself. It isn't

GRAN: 'Mother took such good care of her, but now she's ready for the nursery school.'

good for her. She's too solitary, too selfish. I hope that playing with other children will help her become more sociable and tolerant. But of course all the children in her age group are also single children, so they all share the same character. It isn't easy."

But Jin Jin did have plenty of playmates. The courtyard in front of her house is always full of children and the network of narrow alleyways makes it virtually a traffic-free zone, so Jou Lan has not had to worry about her daughter wandering off into the road. It is also a good place to learn to ride a bike.

Eventually Jou Lan decided that Jin Jin should start attending the day nursery at No 5 Cotton Factory. "While Jin Jin was little I wanted my mother to look after her because she takes such good care of her. But now that she is one she's ready to go to the factory nursery where she can play with other children and learn to be less selfish, to think of other people in everything she does. That's the quality I want to encourage in her."

Jin Jin is in the youngest group, all under two years old. When Jou Lan took her there and said goodbye for the first time, Jin Jin did not want her to go. As her mother left she burst into tears. She had begun to learn that, after the luxury of all that family attention, the world outside was going to be a very different place.

LUNCH: A spoon's easier than chopsticks.   *PLAY: Alleys are traffic-free for bikers.*

SAVITHA: INDIAN AFFAIRS

'I had no idea that my husband and my sister were having a relationship. But it is not good enough. Let the two of them take care of my children as well'

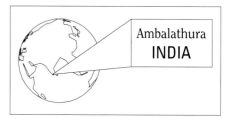

Ambalathura
INDIA

WHEN Savitha was born, her father could not hide his disappointment. His wife Usha had been admitted to hospital more than a week earlier. It had been a difficult labour and he spent many hours waiting on the veranda, wondering why it was taking so long. When the news finally came it was not what he had hoped and prayed for. Usha had given him another daughter. In the tiny community of Ambalathura at the southernmost tip of India, the way the gods answer parents' prayers can affect the rest of their lives. A son is expected to ensure his parents' well-being in life and in death. By tradition, only a son can perform his parents' funeral rights.

In days gone by the birth of a girl might not have worried Chandran so much. Savitha was only his second child after all; the first was a girl called Kochumol. His wife was still young and could bear him many more children. Yet in the state of Kerala, traditional attitudes are having to compromise with modern expectations. The socialist administration has brought in a programme of improved health care, better schools and a highly effective family planning programme, including widespread sterilisation. Volunteer health visitors had often called on Usha and Chandran to offer guidance and quite firm advice. So Chandran had already thought of a way out of his dilemma.

"I wanted a boy," he says. "But I got a girl instead. I am not going to try for a third child because we don't have the economic means to afford another delivery. So when my girls are about three years old I will adopt a boy."

When Usha and Chandran brought Savitha home they were greeted by their whole extended family. Four generations of parents and children, husbands and wives, aunts and uncles all live together in three large huts among the tall coconut palms on the edge of a lagoon. The head of the family is Savitha's great-grandfather Velayudan, a man in his mid seventies with white hair and a white moustache. He had nine sons and only one daughter, who is Usha's mother. All the old man's offspring still live together along with most of their descendants.

Savitha's part of the family live in the smallest hut of the three. Even so, it has to house not only herself, her parents and her sister, Kochumol, but also her two unmarried aunts, Podichi and Bindu, her uncle Murugan, and her grandparents, Thankappan and Nagammal. Savitha's childhood is very much a shared affair, not just because of the close proximity in which they all live. This is a male-dominated family in which Savitha's great-grandfather and increasingly her nine great-uncles, have strong expectations about life in their close-knit community. Very little escapes their attention, and little is private in Usha and Chandran's relationship, or in the way they bring up their children.

Chandran first met Usha when he came to Ambalathura to look for work. Since leaving school he had done many different jobs. For a while he was a 'coolie' or general labourer, then he had been a cow-dung carter. Eventually he settled down to his present trade as a 'dhobi', washing

DISAPPOINTED: Chandran with Usha and Savitha.

clothes. It does not make him much of a living. He says: "Some days I get nothing. On Saturdays I can get about 50 rupees *{about £2}* and I manage with that until the following Saturday. I hope that after two or three months business may pick up and I'll be able to get 25 rupees a day."

Chandran has a lot in common with Usha's family. Many of them also make what little money they can laundering clothes. Their marriage was soon arranged, but Chandran's reasons for marrying Usha were complex. It was partly because he is an eldest son himself and had been under considerable family pressure to arrange his younger sister's marriage, as well as looking after his widowed mother. There was no way that the few rupees he earned from washing clothes would pay his sister's dowry. So he decided to get married.

"I married Usha because I wanted to marry my sister off. I didn't want to sell my house and property to raise the money, because my mother was born there and I want her to die there. I was able to pay for my sister's marriage with the money I got by marrying Usha.

In just the same way, it was quite natural for Chandran to hope that one day in the distant future, his own son might look after his needs. The birth of Savitha did not assure him of that security.

The first few weeks of Savitha's life were mostly spent peacefully in the shade of the hut, resting in the arms of her mother and grandmother. Then it was time for Usha to prepare for an important ceremony.

"Forty-one days after the birth of a child we have the Sacred Thread Ceremony," says Usha. "It's a big celebration and everybody comes – Chandran's mother and his brothers and their wives, as well as my uncles and cousins. We go and buy black thread which we tie around the child's waist. If we don't do this it is bad for the child. The thread protects her from evil. We light a special lamp for the ceremony and we also put the baby in special clothes and give her

CLOSE FAMILY: Four generations all live together in three small huts by the lagoon.

bangles and a silver chain. Then we have a big lunch with rice and curries. Some people, if they are well off, they give their baby a gold chain as well as a silver chain. But we couldn't afford a gold chain."

The ceremony is a success and soon family life in Ambalathura returns to normal. Savitha is beginning to take an interest in her surroundings, closely watching the older children as they play hide and seek among the coconut palms, and listening to her aunt winnowing the rice and her father beating washing in the lagoon. The only sound that disturbs the tranquillity is the raucous cawing of crows nesting above.

Then suddenly one morning the family calm is thrown into turmoil. Usha finds out that Chandran is having an affair with her 18-year-old sister Podichi, has been for some time, and that Podichi is six months pregnant.

"I had no idea that Chandran and Podichi were having a relationship," says Usha. "But it has been going on a long time. We only discovered later that she is pregnant. I suspect it started while I was in hospital having Savitha."

It seems that Chandran and Podichi had tried unsuccessfully to get an abortion. When it became obvious that the family would find out about their affair, Chandran did not have the courage to explain to his parents-in-law. He told a friend, but in a tight community like Ambalathura it did not remain a secret for long. Justice was swiftly handed out by the family. The uncles got together, gave Chandran and Podichi some money for the bus and threw them out. "Once Podichi has had her baby," says Usha, "we will adopt it and get her married off to somebody else."

Usha is naturally devastated at the discovery. She feels betrayed by her sister as well as by her husband, not just because of their affair, but also because she cannot see how she will manage to bring up the children on her own. In her distress she even threatens to take Savitha and Kochumol to Chandran's house and leave them there.

"It is not good enough if the two of them have a good time on their own," she says, high on anger and hurt. "Let them take care of my children as well. If not, let him pay maintenance."

But even as she speaks, she knows inside that she cannot, would not carry out her threat. Every morning as usual, Usha still carefully darkens Savitha's eyebrows with kohl, applies the caste mark and places a tiny black dot on her cheeks to ward off the evil-eye. To Savitha, unaware of the crisis, her mother's touch is the same as ever.

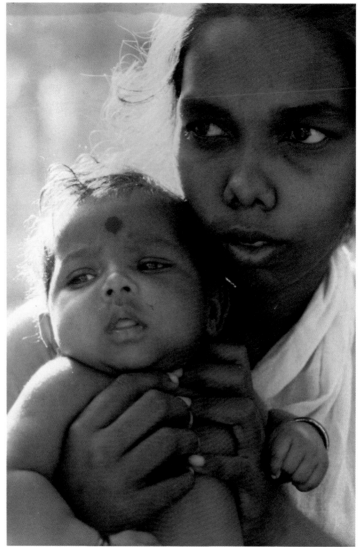

ALONE: *Usha and Savitha. But reconciliation is close.*

Usha insists that she will never take Chandran back. She storms to his house and demands a divorce. He refuses. For a while it looks as though Savitha might lose touch with her father, just when she is becoming attached to him. But Usha would face an impossible struggle trying to bring up her children alone with no guarantees of maintenance from Chandran, and even with the support promised by her uncles.

It is almost inevitable that time and hardship will force reconciliation on them all. It does.

Once Podichi has given birth – to another girl – Usha and Podichi's father, Thankappan, accept mother and daughter back into the household in Ambalathura. There is no question of the uncles allowing Chandran into the community again.

But the simple truth is that Usha and Podichi both need each other. They need each other to work to make enough money to feed their daughters. So while Usha takes laundry for washing, her sister looks after the children. Savitha's life is settled into a new pattern. As she learns to walk she begins to explore the coconut grove around the huts, playing with her older sister, Kochumol, in the soft sandy soil. Aunt Bindu helps look after them both. She says: "Kochumol and Savitha fight sometimes. Savitha takes Kochumol's toys and Kochumol cries and they throw sand over each other's heads. I laugh when I see that. Savitha runs around now and calls mother. Six months ago she just used to drink milk and lie around. Now she plays, walks, holds the wall, stands and breaks anything that she can get."

It is not an easy time for Usha, uncertain about where her future lies, and finding Savitha difficult to manage. She does tend to misbehave, breaking things and throwing her food around. And she is irritable because of an infection on her legs that will not clear up.

"The health clinic gave me some medicine, but it was no good," says Usha. "So I took her to be treated by the witch doctor. He did some magic on a towel and told us to tie it round her legs. She's better now."

Finally, six months after the separation, Chandran sends for Usha, asking her to leave her home in Ambalathura and come to his family's house in nearby Venniyoor. As a young woman in a low-caste community, Usha is caught in a conflict of loyalties between the demand for obedience from her husband and the pressures from her father and uncles. Tired and worn out by it all, she submits to Chandran's request, taking Savitha with her, but leaving her elder daughter Kochumol behind in the care of her sisters. After talking with Chandran's mother and other relatives, Usha and Chandran are reunited. But inevitably tension remains. Usha's family will not accept Chandran back, but nor will they allow her to leave Ambalathura permanently.

Usha finds a compromise. She spends more and more of her time in Venniyoor, but every now and then returns for a few days to Ambalathura. Now that Savitha is talking, her questions suggest she is beginning to understand the complexity of the family relationship and trying to identify her place in it all.

Savitha also has something to look forward to – her mother is pregnant again. A few months after Savitha's second birthday, Usha presents Chandran with another baby. It is a boy.

HANNAH: ELEVENTH IN LINE

'The midwife tells me about foods. Give her vegetables and bananas, she says. But I can't grow them and I can't afford to buy them. She gets maize and beans'

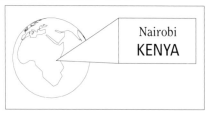

Nairobi
KENYA

STRUGGLE: Grace and Hannah. 'I don't feel joyful, but a birth is always a blessing'

FOR HANNAH early childhood has been one long gamble. She was born into a poor family, even by African standards. Grace and her husband Karanja live in the Kikuyu Highlands, some 45 minutes drive out of Nairobi, Kenya. Like their neighbours, they are subsistence farmers. But this is a densely populated area and there are too many families trying to tease a living out of too little land. It would be an exaggeration to call their place a farm. It is a tiny quarter-acre plot, no bigger than a suburban English garden, on which they try to grow enough food to live.

Childbirth held few surprises for Grace. Hannah's birth was her eleventh – and she is still only 34 years old. Her first girl, Susa Wambui, is now 20, and was born when her mother was little more than a child herself. One of her early babies died of measles at eighteen months, but all the other nine have survived and still live with their parents. There's Monica Wajiko, Nancy Njerji, Jane Warimu, George Gishanga, Joseph Gisheru, Francis Kierje, James Kinuthia and Henry Ndungu. Hannah was named Hannah only when she was baptised. Before that she had been called by her Kikuyu name Wangui. The baptism was a very important ceremony for Hannah's

LIVESTOCK: The family have no cows or goats, just one cat. The skinny chicken died.

FAMILY SNAP: 'I just cared for them as they came along and followed God's teaching.'

family and worth marking with a family photograph. The local photographer was called and all the children lined up in order of height. The family love to pin up their favourite photographs all over the mud walls of their house. This picture has a special place among the collection.

For Grace, baptism is the beginning of a lifelong commitment. She will do everything she can to make sure that Hannah attends church and Sunday school every week throughout her childhood and beyond.

"I am happy when the children go to the service at church because they'll be taught good behaviour and they'll learn how to look after themselves in a better way. While they stay with the church they won't get mixed up with others who don't know about God.

"I train my children by telling them when they do wrong, telling them when they have made a mistake. Sometimes if I have to repeat the same thing again and again, then I beat them with the carpet cane, or I ask one of the oldest girls to do it. Then I don't have to repeat the same thing again. I don't think children are beginning to grow up until they understand the difference between right and wrong."

As a young mother Grace never wondered how many children she would have or how she would manage to bring them all up. "I just cared for them as they came along and followed God's teaching."

She knew little about birth control until quite recently. Children were born when God wished it. But after her tenth pregnancy she had believed there would be no more and viewed the prospect of an eleventh with stoical resignation. "I don't feel joyful. But the birth of a child is always a blessing. If God helps, one more won't be a big problem. But this is the last. With all the problems we have now, I want no more babies."

For Grace, bringing up another child is a struggle to provide those bare necessities of clean water to drink, enough food to eat and at least one set of second-hand clothes to wear. She is a regular visitor to the well-equipped Lusigeti Health Clinic and Hannah was given her first immunization dose there within hours of birth.

"The doctor tells me my children are getting better and better. On the scales Hannah is much heavier than Susa was at the same age. She is even beginning to walk at only eight months."

Hannah did have a difficult start, though. As a baby, she caught malaria and was in hospital for two months. Grace stayed with her throughout, while the older girls shared the housework and cooking back at home. Jane remembers: "Hannah fell sick while we were in school. By the time we came back home she had already been taken to the hospital and mummy was not at home. We were very worried and wondered what had happened to our child, because we really loved her. When our father finally brought them back home two months later, we were very happy, because we had thought that our child was going to die."

Even when Hannah is back home, life is very hard on Grace. She has been taught at the Clinic how to feed and care for her babies properly, what are the essentials for their diet and what will happen to them if they do not get the right foods. But that knowledge does not pay for the food. It simply means that Grace knows what her children are having to miss out on through the family's poverty.

Every day she works on their tiny plot, and a neighbour also lets her cultivate another quarter-acre nearby. If the weather is kind Grace can harvest two crops a year. During the November rains she plants beans and potatoes, and once these are harvested in the New Year she plants maize. But even with two crops a year Grace cannot possibly feed the ten children who are dependent on her.

"At the clinic the midwife tells me all the good foods the children should eat. 'Give them vegetables and bananas,' she says. But I can't grow vegetables here because we don't have enough water to take care of them. And I can't go out and buy vegetables for my children because I don't have the money. My crops of maize and beans aren't something you can sell in the market, so I just have to use them to feed my children."

Whenever she can Grace goes out to work on other women's farms, earning a few shillings a day. But despite all the hard work the children are never far from danger.

"It's very difficult because sometimes I'm not able to feed my children. They have to go to sleep hungry. Other times they must go naked because I don't have enough blankets to cover them. So I do find it hard to care for my children. Often I go out to look for jobs, but mostly I come back with nothing. It is difficult."

The family used to live in a traditional grass house but then Karanja's brother who lived nearby decided to move away and offered them his modern three-roomed wattle and daub house with a pitched corrugated-iron roof. They pulled it apart, carted it and re-built it on their plot. It is simple but adequate. There is no floor other than the bare, dusty, red earth on which sit a rough table and chairs, sleeping mats and a couple of trestle beds. There is a lean-to kitchen on one side of the house with an open wood fire and a few basic cooking pots. There is no electricity and most of life goes on outside the house. From the moment she could sit unsupported, Hannah has spent most of her time on that red earth, where her brothers and sisters have also learned to sit, crawl and walk.

Hannah's is a small world, and she hardly ever leaves their plot of land, except for the Sunday walk to church and those days when Grace takes Hannah with her to work on some neighbour's field.   While Hannah's mother works, her father spends much of his day sitting in the shade at the side of his house. Karanja is much older than Grace and not a strong man. He is often ill, aggravated by the dry red dust that is blown about by the stifling summer winds. Even if he were well it is unlikely that he would do much to help grow the food to feed his family. Cultivation is traditionally women's work and he has more or less given up trying to get any different sort of a job either, standing little chance against younger men with far more schooling than he ever had.

As a boy he was given by his father to a tribe of wandering Masai herdsmen, probably in repayment of a debt. They taught him how to look after cattle, but he and Grace have no cows nor even a goat. They had a skinny chicken once, but it died. Now they just have their pets, which are more of a drain than a resource. There is a pathetically thin dog, which lies all day out in front of the house, and a cat which Hannah likes to tease and cuddle.

In days gone by Hannah would have been looked after almost exclusively by her older brothers and especially sisters, releasing their mother to work except at feeding times. But the modern demand that children go to school has changed all that.

"I usually take Hannah with me, mostly because once the others are in school there's nobody left to care for her," says Grace. "With the children at school I have a lot to do, minding the baby and trying to cook for everyone, as well as working."

Even so, in the morning and after school, the older children have been expected to help a great deal during Hannah's infancy, not only looking after their youngest sister, but collecting water, cleaning pots, washing clothes and cooking. As eleven-year-old Jane Warimu explains: "When we wake up in the morning we pray, then sweep the house, wash the dishes and light the fire. I put on the water to wash, then we wake the younger ones. By that time we've left water for making tea on the fire. Once we have finished dressing, six of us go to school.

"When we see mother is tired, we take Hannah, wash her, oil her and dress her. Before dressing her, we feed her so that she doesn't pour food on her clothes. Then we carry her while she sleeps, and while she plays I start knitting a sweater."

As Hannah approaches her second birthday, she is growing more and more independent.

Jane says: "Hannah won't let anyone give her food. If we try to feed her, she takes it from her mouth and throws it away. But she is trying to help us now. If we're washing the dishes, she starts bringing them and putting them where the rest are being washed. If we ask for something she brings it to us. When she is given her toy dog she covers it with a towel and then says she will feed it from her breasts. Then she tries to tie it on to her back like our mother used to carry her. That makes us all laugh."

In a few years she will join her older brothers and sisters at the Lusigeti Primary School. Classes are large, there are not enough books or equipment and prospects are poor. But that is all in the future. For the time being Hannah is more interested in sharing in the daily task of cultivating the maize on which her next meal depends.

SZABOLCS: ACCORDING TO PLAN

'We'd like a large family, but there has to be an upper limit. In this small apartment we just couldn't cope with more than two'

Budapest
HUNGARY

SZABOLCS showed a good sense of timing. He was born on the eve of Hungary's Constitution Day, so his four-year-old sister Vanda could celebrate by going down to the banks of the Danube with her father Istvan to watch the spectacular firework display.

Hungary has an impressive maternity system. Because there is so much concern about the declining birth rate, healthy babies are a national priority, and Szabolcs was born in one of Budapest's biggest maternity hospitals. He was delivered into the hands of an obstetrician, who passed him immediately over to be thoroughly cleaned under a powerful shower. Still spluttering and gurgling, he was then weighed and measured, checked for malformations and wrapped in white linen. Then and only then was he presented to Agnes, his mother. It had been a straightforward birth at the end of a normal pregnancy. In most Hungarian hospitals, relatives are not allowed into the delivery room, so Agnes faced the birth alone.

"Compared with Vanda it was a much quicker birth," she says. "But it was harder and hurt a lot more. Even so, everything soon seemed beautiful, especially as the baby was a boy."

Szabolcs's birth completed the family plans for Agnes and Istvan. Now they have a boy and a girl, even if Vanda is not too sure about the idea: "I was expecting a girl," she says. "I don't want a boy because the boys at kindergarten fight. A brother will mean more cars to play with, but a sister means more dolls."

But once Vanda met her baby brother, she changed her mind and was eager to tell him all about their home and family as they drove back to their apartment on the Buda side of the river Danube. It is very small by British standards, but typical of accommodation available to young couples in Budapest, including professional people with relatively good incomes, such as Agnes and Istvan. They have only one main room, with their sleeping area curtained off at one end. There is a tiny kitchen and bathroom, but Vanda has the only bedroom, which she will now share with her brother. The house is well furnished, with plenty of books, records and a television. But there is little space for lively youngsters to play. Outside is not much better, with only a small patch of grass separating the entrance from the trams, buses and other traffic that constantly pass up and down the busy street. While they live in that apartment, the children will have to spend all their days indoors, except when Agnes or Istvan take them for their daily walk down to the nearby playground. Such restrictions weighed heavily on Istvan's mind.

"We both love children very much," he says. "We'd like to have a large family. But there has to be an upper limit. In this small apartment, we just couldn't cope with more than two. We've also reached the stage with Vanda when we can all do things together. We go out for the day, take holidays, go skiing. Obviously with a new baby it will be a while before we can do things like that.

"At the same time we think that Vanda needs to have a little sister or brother. For four years she has been growing up as an only child, and this shows in her behaviour and thinking, despite having been with other children at kindergarten. So for over half a year now, we've been systematically preparing Vanda for the birth. We have been teaching her that she will have to share her toys, her room and everything with the second child. And we have been teaching her about how babies are born. We were worried about how she would react, but she has gradually become accustomed to the idea."

Agnes and Istvan were also trying to balance their desire for a family against the demands of their work. Agnes is a computer programmer for a firm of transport engineers and

PLAY: 'I can't give much time to the children. I have to work.'

Istvan works in an industrial development bank. "One of the main considerations is that we both have professions, and a large family causes a lot of problems, requires much time, and of course it means a certain nervous strain. Agnes spent two years at home after Vanda was born, which was good. But once Vanda had started at kindergarten, Agnes was doing so well in her work that we had difficulty deciding when the next child should come. As a matter of fact, we planned it for a little earlier, but one or two months' delay doesn't matter."

Agnes was trying to work out how best to organise her time after the birth. "Originally we thought that I'd stay at home for just one year," she says. "But now I think I'll probably stay at home for two years. In Hungary we get a maternity payment for three months, followed by a children's allowance for three years, which is financially quite good. So it makes sense to stay at home rather than send the baby to a child care centre, plus the enjoyment of having the child at home."

Most Hungarian mothers go back to work soon after their babies are born, out of choice or necessity. Now, with Vanda at kindergarten much of the day, Szabolcs can enjoy much more of his mother's attention. Istvan, too, has spent more time with his son than many fathers, especially during the early months when Szabolcs was given the same meticulous care and attention that they apply to every aspect of their lives. One corner of their room was set up as a nappy-changing area with a full range of creams and lotions. Istvan's job included giving Szabolcs his bath as soon as he got home from work. Like all parents they have been under the guidance of a paediatrician, who visited the home and gave Szabolcs a full developmental check-up.

Once Szabolcs was toddling, father and son took walks in the park together as often as Istvan could spare the time. But this has been getting more and more difficult.

"I have a lot of work. I start at 8.30 and must really do my best if I am to finish everything by 6.00 in the evening. And when I get home I can't give much time to the children. My working hours aren't specified. My work is mainly task-orientated. But it takes an awful lot of time to get everything done."

The demands of work were also worrying Agnes. With the most intensive period of caring for Szabolcs behind her, she was keen to begin picking up the threads of her professional life and began to take on small pieces of work to do at home. She bought a play-pen for Szabolcs, but he did not think much of the idea of losing his companion to a computer.

"I find I can't do the work when Szabolcs is around," says Agnes. "He always wants to sit on my lap or play on the computer keyboard, so I can't concentrate. I prefer to work when the children have gone to bed. Then I go on until eleven or midnight."

When Vanda is at home, things are different. They have become the best of friends – most of the time.

"Vanda adores Szabolcs. I think she likes her little brother more than is normal in children her age. Perhaps when she grows up she'll choose to work with little children, I don't know. There have been no problems of jealousy, although we have noticed now that Szabolcs is starting to move around, and show an interest in her things, Vanda has become a little more self-willed and less obedient. I think she has suddenly realised that Szabolcs is going to be with us forever. But mostly they get on very well. It's Vanda who can really make him laugh. They romp about and roar with laughter together."

With Szabolcs approaching his second birthday, Agnes decided he was ready to go to kindergarten and she was ready to resume full time work.

"He was getting bored at home," she says. "He missed the other children. He wanted to go and play with our neighbour's boy who is the same age, but has already started nursery. He only had me for company all day and it wasn't enough for him. So he started nursery at 21 months."

Hungary has a long tradition of providing quality child care centres, and Szabolcs's nursery is no exception. Agnes stayed with him several days before she left him for the first time. Even so settling in was not easy.

"It was quite terrible at first, listening through the door waiting for him to finish crying. But I knew I couldn't go in. That wouldn't have been good for him. It took quite a few days, but I knew he would get used to it."

With their family complete, Szabolcs at nursery and Vanda at school, Agnes and Istvan are relatively free to pursue their professional careers. They feel that it is a good compromise. Agnes says: "I believe that without children the family is not a real family. It has its advantages,

OUTING: 'We used to go skiing together. It will be quite a while before we can again.'

of course. Without children we could move much more freely, whereas having children imposes a serious restriction on our time – especially when they're small.

"But I wouldn't feel I had led a full life without children. A child is absolutely not an investment, it is a source of joy and happiness. I mean, I have to bring up a child. I want to create surroundings that will help him develop normally. I want to teach him everything that I think is worth knowing."

Agnes and Istvan are very aware of the unequal opportunities that will affect their children in the future. "Right now in our present society I think boys are in an advantaged position. I mean, statistically speaking they are. But in my opinion being a boy or girl should make no difference. What matters is their abilities and attitudes, their intelligence and humanity. It should really be a question of what people are capable of."

CHAPTER TWO: HEALTH

NEETU AND AZIZ: CRUSADERS

'If we find that children have not been given BCG, polio and triple antigens vaccinations, we bring them to the clinic'

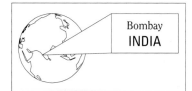

Bombay
INDIA

***FRONT LINE:** 'We check fingers, toes, armpits, bellies and bottoms of children under five.'*

THE CHILDREN of Bombay are on the march with banners unfurled, songs, dances and a zeal to make any revolutionary proud. They are the front-line fighters in a war that is sweeping the country, a war against malnutrition and the diseases that kill and cripple children under five. They are the Health Detectives and their crusade is taking immunization into the slums where so many have died.

Two of these new warriors are eleven-year-old Neetu and Aziz, who live in the stinking slum called Malvani, home for 100,000 on the northern outskirts of Bombay.

Aziz says: "When we go on an immunization march we carry banners, sing, dance and chant. Then we act a play. Afterwards, we visit each and every family. We leave our sandals outside and then we greet the family. Then we ask permission to enter. We ask if they have any children below five years of age. For such children we want to know whether they have been vaccinated

ACTION: 'We carry banners, sing, dance, chant and act a play. Then we visit the families.'

against BCG, polio, triple antigens, and so on. If we find that the children were not given these vaccinations, we help in bringing them to the clinic."

Today the sight of Neetu, Aziz and their friends marching through the community is less common than it used to be. Their success has been so great that when they conducted a survey of babies in Malvani they found that nearly all had been immunised. They had got the message through.

So they turned next to the diarrhoea conditions that weaken and dehydrate small children in Malvani, especially during the monsoon. They soon mastered the technique known as oral rehydration therapy, as Neetu explains: "If we come across an unhealthy child we inquire whether the child has had diarrhoea. If yes we tell them how to prepare a syrup solution. The recipe is: take a glass of boiled water, add two spoonfuls of sugar, a pinch of salt, a pinch of bicarbonate of soda and half a lemon. We give this to the patient."

Neetu is also an expert on the diagnosis and treatment of scabies, a parasite that buries under the skin causing rashes and infection.

"We examine children for scabies. We look at their skin, especially where the limbs are in close contact. We check their fingers, toes, armpits, bellies and bottoms. If they have got scabies they have a rash and do a lot of scratching. If we find this we bring the whole family to the clinic and let them take a bath with BB solution." BB stands for benzyl benzonate. The children watch while a nurse administers a low concentration solution and then they lead their young patient outside to dry in the sun. Their work on scabies, too, has been a remarkable success. When these young child health workers made their first surveys of scabies in 1978, they found 477 cases. By 1985 there were only 21. Conducting surveys to monitor the incidence of disease has been an important part of Aziz and Neetu's training. More recently, they have been tackling another common complaint among Malvani's young – anaemia. Aziz says: "To diagnose anaemia we examine their gums, their tummy, their forehead and their eyes. We look for any spots in their eyes. We look for unhealthy gums and mouth sores. We examine bleeding gums. We look to see if the nails, the tongue and the eyes are white or not. Having seen these signs, we bring the patient to the clinic. We take a drop of his blood, put it in a tube and add a few drops of water to see whether it becomes 10 grams or less. If we suspect anaemia, we prescribe green vegetables, gram {chick-peas} and jaggery {palm sugar}."

Neetu and Aziz each look after a small group of families, as Neetu explains: "I have six families that I take special care of. My own family and five neighbours. I tell them about diseases, such as anaemia, about deficiencies of vitamin A, vitamin B, vitamin C, vitamin D and protein. Also about tuberculosis."

Child-to-Child schemes were pioneered by David Morley and colleagues at the Institute Of Child Health in London, and are now running throughout the world. The Malvani scheme started ten years ago when the slum had an appalling record of death and disease among babies and young children. There was a health clinic but the doctors and nurses were already overstretched and their attempts to communicate quite simple child health messages about vaccination and nutrition were having little impact. One of the problems was the layout of Malvani itself. Small huts, mostly made of timber and tin are laid out in tidy rows, so closely packed that no vehicle can pass through. It was full of poverty and disease, but impenetrable.

Neetu describes life in Malvani. "I live with my mother and father and two younger brothers. We are flanked by houses on both sides. After two alleys there is a latrine. Malvani has many diseases because of all the rubbish all around. The gutters remain dirty. They're not cleaned. People don't wash themselves and also people spread the rubbish around instead of collecting it in a bin."

Neetu's family also have to collect all their water from one of the communal taps, which only work for two short sessions a day. One unmistakable feature of Malvani life is the stench. There are open drains along every street which run into great arteries of disease that feed the whole community. In the dry season they become the resting place for waste of all descriptions which festers in the blistering heat, untouched except by the dogs and small children. Then, once the monsoon downpours drench the town, these drains overflow, washing their sordid contents back into the muddy streets and turning them into a quagmire of filth.

One scheme the doctors and health workers tried was to provide free school meals for children which they hoped to combine with lessons in nutrition for mothers. But although mothers accepted the free meals gladly, they seemed less enthusiastic about showing up themselves. So the organisers jokingly threatened the children that their meals would be stopped unless more mothers joined in the scheme. No mother, no meal, they said. The impact was immediate. Attendance rates shot up. Ordinary children had got a message through where highly-trained professionals had failed. So, the doctors thought, if it has worked once why not expand it? Let children themselves be the health messengers. They are keen, they know their own community, they are not threatening or frightening as doctors can be, and their energies are freely available. If the parents object to being told what to do by children, they do not show it. They seem grateful for the help.

There is nothing new about children caring for children. For thousands of years, children have played a major role in the day-to-day care of others just a few years younger than themselves. Children in the Malvani Primary School were already getting some lessons on health. Now these were extended, and supple-

SLUM: 'Malvani has many diseases because of the rubbish.'

mented with activities during weekends and holidays. The children welcomed these activities, finding that practical teaching about everyday health problems, diagnosis, treatment and prevention was much more interesting than learning from text-books.

"We learn about all these things by playing games at the Health Centre," says Aziz. "There's Pass The Parcel, Dog And Bone and family games. We spend an hour twice a week on the Child Care programme. And I finish my homework early to be able to go and work in the community."

Child-to-Child is impressive in its coverage. One hundred young health messengers such as Neetu and Aziz, each caring for six families, can monitor the health of well over a thousand small children with a frequency of contact and an intimacy that not even the best-funded health service could equal.

The scheme is rewarding for Neetu and Aziz, too. The quality of their learning about health has washed over into other lessons and they have gained confidence through the responsibility given to them. The knowledge they have gained will stay with them and better equip them to become more effective parents, and might even help them become adult health workers themselves later on. Neetu for one is already clear about her priorities: "Why do we do it?" she says. "Because we're thinking about others."

KAVITA:VICTIM OF POLIO

'I had to have callipers fitted. They were very weighty when I tried to walk. I like hopscotch and ball, but I can't run. I fall down if I try to'

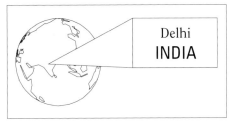

Delhi
INDIA

"MY NAME is Kavita. I study at the Amar Jyoti school for disabled children. I became ill one day with a headache. When my mummy tried to stand me up I fell down. She took me to a doctor and he told us that I had been struck with polio."

If there had been a Child-to-Child project in the suburb of Delhi where Kavita lives, she might be walking properly today. Instead, for want of a routine vaccination in infancy she is condemned to stumble through the rest of her life with her legs locked in heavy iron callipers.

"I had to have callipers fitted on my legs. They were very heavy at first. I could not lift my legs. They felt very weighty when I tried to walk. I like to study and play. I like hopscotch and ball. But I can't run. I fall down if I try to.

"The doctor examined my leg and told my uncle that I should be given callipers and that he should come and get them. My mother helped me to walk with them and my teachers did the same at school. I started by using a wall for support and learned to move slowly. Later I

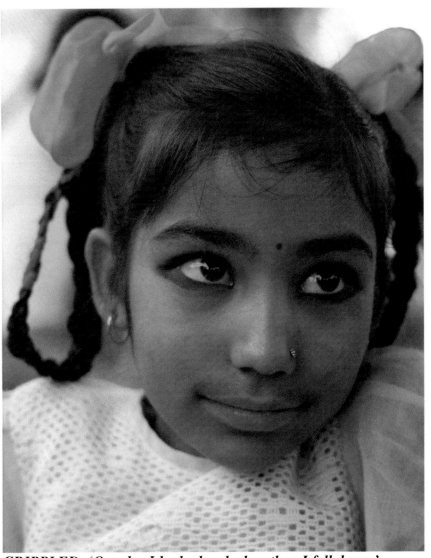

CRIPPLED: 'One day I had a headache...then I fell down.'

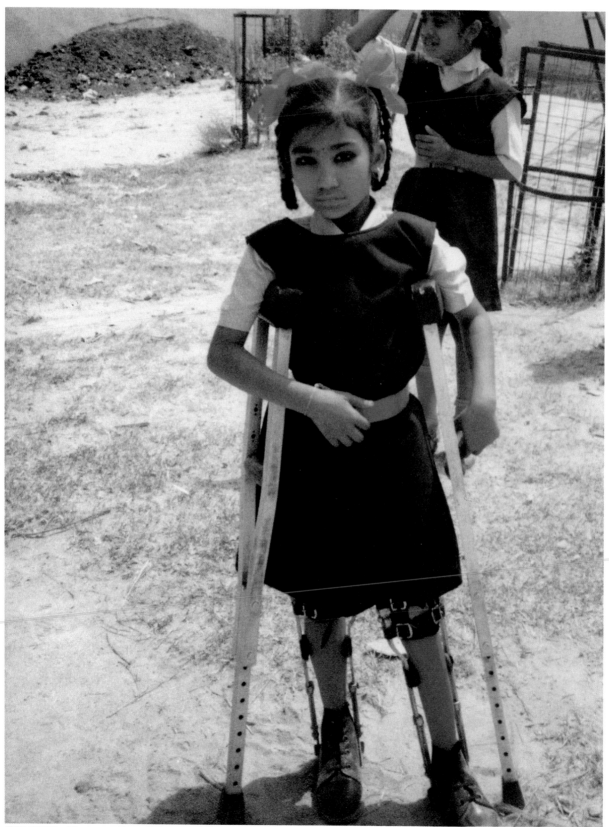

BRAVE: *'I started walking using a wall for support. It took a very long time.'*

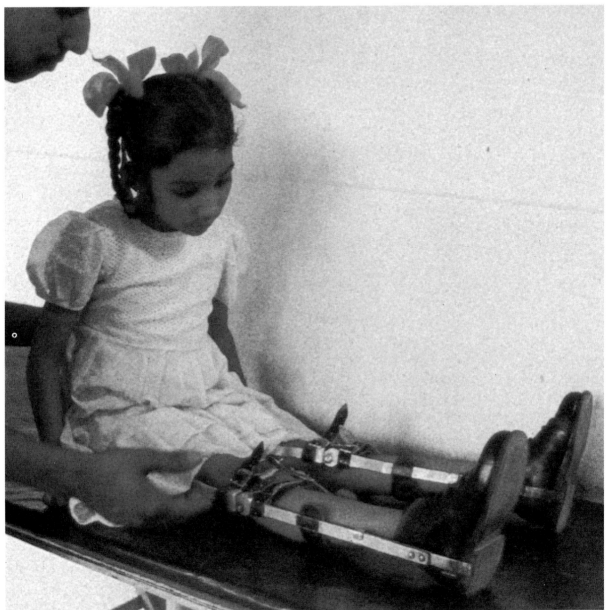

VERDICT: 'The doctor examined my leg and told my uncle that I should have callipers.'

was given crutches. It took a very long time." The fact that Kavita caught polio was not due to any particular negligence by her family. It was simply due to a lack of information. Kavita's grandmother explains: "Before all this happened we didn't know about the anti-polio treatment – that if when she was little Kavita had been given a vaccination she wouldn't have got polio. We had no idea.

"She was watching television when she started running a temperature. She said she had a headache. I went to fetch something from the doctor. I brought some medicine from him so she was all right for the rest of the day. The following morning her mummy got her up and tried to make her stand – but she just fell down.

"We didn't know what could be the matter with her – just overnight she had lost the use of her legs. The day before she had been walking and running about, but by the morning she couldn't

THE SCOURGE OF POLIO

Polio has been crippling children for centuries. Its effects were depicted in the temple drawings of Ancient Egypt. The poliomyelitis virus is spread through contaminated food and water. Initial cold-like symptoms, fever, vomiting and diarrhoea lead to muscle stiffness and pain and eventually paralysis.

The disease destroys the motor nerve cells of the spinal cord, causing the paralysis and leading to progressive wasting of unused muscles.

During the 1950s there were severe epidemics in the USA and Europe, but in these parts of the world the disease has been controlled by universal vaccination since the 1960s.

Three doses of oral vaccination in infancy, at 6, 10 and 14 weeks, are usually all it takes to guard against the disease and protect growing limbs. Yet every year a quarter of a million small children still fall victim to polio. Around 25,000 of them die and many more are crippled for life.

even stand up. I took her to the doctor in Karolbagh {East Delhi}. The doctor told me she had polio, then I brought her back and took her to another doctor in Shahdara. This doctor also said she had polio. I mean to say that we kept on trying to get help, but it was all no use. She had polio so her legs had become completely weak. She became unable to walk.

"So we took her to Meerut, a town not far from Delhi, and she stayed in hospital there for two whole months. She was being treated there. But we ran out of money to pay for the treatment. So we brought her back home again. We ordered callipers for her and she began to stand a little with those – they cost 200 rupees. Then after that we heard about Amar Jyoti. We took her to their clinic and filled in the application forms for the school."

Kavita is fortunate in being able to attend the school run by the Amar Jyoti voluntary organisation. The school integrates handicapped with able-bodied pupils, on the same principle as Child-to-Child – letting children themselves help each other. Kavita has one very special friend: "Renu has been my friend since I joined the school three and a half years ago."

Sadly, Kavita's experience is far from being rare. It has been estimated that at least one child in ten is born or becomes physically or mentally handicapped.

ELIZABETH: A PERFECT SMILE

'About half the kids in my grade have stuff in their mouths – retainers or bases or stuff like that. It doesn't hurt, but you can't eat very chewy things'

New York
U.S.A.

ELIZABETH'S health concerns have nothing to do with too little to eat or with crippling childhood diseases. She lives in New York City and health care to her means having her teeth straightened. She is one of the three and a half million Americans receiving orthodontic treatment at any one time. In a country where millions of dollars are spent each year on cosmetic surgery, the rapidly-growing orthodontics industry has been able to tap a vast market.

SMILE: But it was not perfect enough.

Once only a handful of children needed to wear a brace. But today, more and more, it is being accepted as a normal – almost inevitable – part of growing up.

Good teeth does not mean healthy teeth, but perfect, straight, gleaming white teeth. Toothpaste commercials and the great Hollywood grin have turned the nation's head. The uniqueness of each individual, including a few minor irregularities is being replaced by technical perfection – a Barbie-doll image of uniformity.

Walk into any Junior High School classroom in one of the wealthy suburbs and as many as six out of ten children will be wearing a brace. Their mouths are filled with orthodontic scaffolding, their teeth tightly harnessed – all in the cause of looking good. Now it is Elizabeth's turn.

"I'm 11 and I live close by Central Park in the middle of New York City. Tomorrow I'm going to the orthodontist to get braces and something in my palate to help straighten my teeth. I think it's going to hurt a little bit. I'm going to get screws stuck in my teeth and then they'll put on the brace and that will start moving my teeth and jaw.

"I don't think it's going to be very comfortable in my mouth and I'm not going to be able to remove it at any time. So it's going to be hard to brush my teeth and I'm not going to be able to

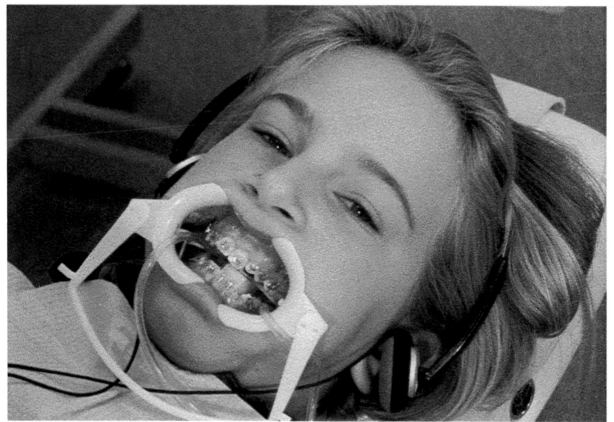

TREATMENT: 'I had screws stuck in my teeth and then a brace to move them.'

eat very chewy things. I don't think it's going to be that good." In the end, it did not hurt Elizabeth too much. Her orthodontist is one of the most highly regarded in Manhattan. His waiting room is lavishly furnished, not that Elizabeth and her mother were expected to wait there for long. They were soon led into the designer surgery, all green plastic panelling. And if that was not enough to distract Elizabeth from the wiring-up, she was provided with a personal video showing the latest cartoons.

"It didn't hurt or anything, so it was pretty good. First they put some junk on my teeth, some glue, stuff like that. Then they put little pieces of metal on that stuff, so they stuck on my teeth. Then they put on the wires. They're sort of pressing on my teeth, but it's not too bad."

The fitting complete, Elizabeth was presented with her free gift – a yellow T-shirt with the slogan: Braces Are Beautiful. She has a good many months to convince herself of the truth in that message. And even after the brace itself is removed, she will have to wear a retainer until her teeth have settled down. So she will be visiting the orthodontist many times over the next two years. But she takes having to wear a brace for granted.

"About half the kids in my grade have stuff in their mouths – bases or retainers or stuff like that."

It will all cost Elizabeth's parents anything up to £4,000 for the treatment. They, at least, feel that it's a fair price to pay for a perfect smile.

MATTHEW: THE BURGER KING

'Mom says if I lose 30 or 40 pounds, she'll buy me a scooter, a football, a baseball set and a basketball. I have to keep going'

New York U.S.A.

MATTHEW is a victim of malnutrition. He loves to ride his bike, but he is out of breath by the end of the street. He loves to play basketball, but he is so slow he rarely gets anywhere near the ball. He loves to climb trees, but never gets higher than the bottom branches. When he goes shopping with his mum he has trouble finding clothes that fit. When he is at school, he looks gross on the undersize chairs. Already at ten years old, he does not look good and he does not feel good. And it is not likely to get better as he gets older. Three out of every four obese children become obese adults, with a greater risk of strokes and heart attacks, high blood pressure and hypertension, hernias and diabetes – the list goes on and on.

Matthew's kind of malnutrition is very different from haunting images of starving children. But it is malnutrition just the same, and it is commonplace in the richest nation on earth. An excess of fats and sugar is one of the greatest hazards. American children consume an average of 2 pounds of sugar each a week. Their eating habits are shaped early, not least by TV commercials. Matthew has spent a lot of his childhood lying around on the sofa watching TV, and he knows the jingles off by heart – about fabulous fruities, miracle munchies and sparkling snacks.

Kids' TV in the USA is big business for the food corporations. Out of all the adverts, 75 per cent are for food products, especially sugar-saturated breakfast cereals. Many of the cereals are 50 per cent sugar. And then the kids are taught to put yet more sugar on top. Matthew has been a receptive target for high-pressure selling, ever since he was tiny.

Now his mum and dad realise there is a problem, and they are trying to get Matthew started on a diet.

"My Mom says: 'If you keep on eating like that, one day you'll trip over at the top of a hill, and roll all the way down to the bottom.' Guess who got her into saying that? My Dad. He doesn't like me getting fat. He says I have to lose weight: 'You wanna exercise or go on a diet to get this weight off,' he says. He says it's for my own good. I don't want to be like this all my life – it'd be weird."

But Matthew's favourite dinner is a Big Burger with a side order of fries, and plenty of ketchup. The big fast food companies spend millions of dollars each year on advertising. That's tough on Matthew, especially when other kids make fun of him.

"Sometimes at school other kids tease me. They say: 'Hey, Fatty!' When they call me fat I say: 'I know I'm fat so don't start bothering me about it.' And sometimes fat kids call me fat. So I say to them: 'Why do you call me fat? Remember next time to look at yourself before you call somebody fat'."

One of the problems is that Matthew is crazy about sport, especially basketball, and he looks forward to games at school.

TAUNTS: 'Kids tease me. They say: "Hey, Fatty!" I don't want to be like this all my life.'

"We learn how to throw the basketball and how to dribble. We learn how to run with the basketball, and how to throw it straight, and get it into the hoop. When I run fast, real fast, I get tired because I have asthma."

For Matthew, trying to lose weight is going to be a long uphill struggle. His mum has made all sorts of promises, but how do you tell a ten-year-old he is not allowed all his most favourite foods?

"My Mom says if lose about 30 or 40 pounds before school ends, that she might buy me a scooter, a football, a baseball set and a basketball; all that stuff she'll buy me if I lose weight. That's why I have to keep going."

Matthew still hangs on to his dreams of a slim, sporting future, but he seems to know that they are unlikely to come to much. "I want to be a quarterback when I grow up. It'd be fun. But I don't know what the future has in store for me."

DAVID: FIGHTING A HANDICAP

'I does reading, number, dinner time, writing, library. I do the clock, check the register, tidy the books – lots of things'

Staffordshire
ENGLAND

JOHN and Marg live in Tamworth, Staffordshire, with sons David, 9, and Christopher, 6. David is Down's Syndrome. About 1 child in 700 is born with Down's Syndrome. It is caused by a genetic abnormality, in most cases an extra chromosome 21. Down's Syndrome children have poor muscle control and are susceptible to respiratory and heart conditions. The extent of their learning difficulties varies. An increasing proportion are being integrated into ordinary schools.

SON: 'We're proud of David. He really tries.'

'MY NAME is David. I go to a special school. I work hard. I does reading, number, dinner time, writing, library – have books there. I do the clock, check the register, tidy up the book corner, then give the drinks out. Lots of things. Washing car, we got sponges and bucket. Then got the soap wet, we did. After that I put the hose on. I dried it off, then put the car in the garage, lock it in, make sure the door's locked, the windows. Then make a cup of tea.

Football. Football's the best. I like Manchester United. I get the ball, pretend I'm Bryan Robson. I like Mark Hughes and Brian McClair, too. I kick it up and down, up and down, up and down, in the net, on the grass. My brother can head it. I can't do that, hurts my head – header might hurt me. I just want to kick the ball in the net. Then I shout 'Yeah'.'

David's parents talk about life with him.
JOHN: "The experience of having David has changed our attitude completely. I always thought when I saw a handicapped child: 'I could never cope with something like that. That wouldn't happen to me.'

"It has done, and you can cope, and things aren't so bad. Obviously, being our first

GOAL: 'Football's best. I just want to kick the ball in the net. Then I shout: Yeah!'

child, it was very exciting. I didn't know what to expect. I thought the birth went fantastic. I shed a tear when I saw it was a boy, and rushed off to phone the family. But when I got back, I remember the paediatrician coming in and saying: 'I believe your baby is mongoloid.' I think that was what she said, because had she said 'Down's Syndrome' we probably wouldn't have known what she meant. I can remember how I felt. It was a sort of numbness. It was a bombshell. I had to go back to the phone again and tell our parents: 'Yes, we've got a boy, but he's handicapped.'

MARG: "I was only 25, and they always say it only happens in older women. I felt very alone, as though nobody else in the world had got a handicapped baby."

JOHN: "We had genetic counselling. We had to go to the hospital to meet with this, I think it was a Professor something. My impression was that he was firing statistics at us, telling us we were one-in-so-many, and if we had another child, the chances would be one-in-so-many again. I thought at the time, we didn't need that sort of thing, so soon after having David. The worst thing was our ignorance of mental handicap. At first we hadn't got a clue what David was going to be like. But David is his own character, his own personality. He's good, he's bad, he cries, he laughs. And that's just like anyone else."

MARG: "David has done everything, but he's done it slowly. You know, he's reached milestones later than a normal child. When Christopher came along, he did everything within his milestones. I think by now, Christopher's probably overtaken David. Now, Christopher is helping David's development. Before we had Christopher, David wasn't very imaginative. But Christopher's taught him how to play and use his imagination more. Like, when they play at schools. Well, obviously Christopher's the teacher, he tends to be the one that does the reading and writing and he tries to help David. Mind you, they do swap over and David will pretend to mark the register and then he'll say: 'I'm taking it to the office' which is what he does at school. Playing like that has really brought him out."

JOHN: "One thing we've noticed about David is his ability to absorb fine detail. He always seems to watch people, and pick out little things that we wouldn't even notice. Like watching athletes on TV, David can mimic the guy doing the long jump, all his little mannerisms, right from the moment he steps on to the track. It's the same thing with anything he watches. When we've been watching football on TV and then we go out for a game, the boys are always hugging and kissing when they score a goal, just like the professionals do. I've always loved football, and the thought of having a son who'd be interested in football was everything to me. When we had David I was elated. My first thought was: 'We'll be out kicking a ball together.' Now Christopher's come along and his interest in football has rubbed off on David, which is lovely to see. Sometimes I have to say to Christopher: 'Come on, let your brother have a kick, let's even it up a little bit.' But there's no favouritism, I've got two boys and they're praised when they're good, they're chastised when they're naughty and there's no difference at all."

MARG: "Christopher cares a lot about his big brother. Obviously they fall out like any other brothers, but I hope he'll continue to love David and care for him. Christopher will have his own life to lead, and he'll be encouraged to do so, as long as he cares for his brother, which I think he will. We're very proud of David, especially for things he's achieved in school. Things you'd probably take for granted in a normal child, take David a long time, but he really tries to do them, and he succeeds in the end."

CHAPTER THREE: HOME

RICHIE: A DOUBLE DIVORCE

'Daddy Tommy is my real dad, but it seems like Daddy Roger is more my dad because I used to see him more. I don't know...it's kind of strange'

New York
U.S.A.

LIKE every good all-American boy, Richie loves his mother. He also loves BOTH his fathers. Even when it all gets a little confusing for a ten-year-old.

Richie's mother Carol split up from his father, Tommy, when Richie was just six months old. Carol remarried and Richie was brought up by her new husband, Roger, a man Richie also learned to call Daddy. Now Carol and Roger have divorced, too.

So a bewildered Richie lives alone with his mother in the bustle of New York, with frequent visits from both his fathers. He calls them Daddy Tommy and Daddy Roger, just to keep things simple.

Richie tries to make some sense of it all: "Well, my Daddy Tommy is my real dad, but it seems like Daddy Roger is more my dad because I used to see him more. But now it seems like they're equal...or something. I don't know...it's kind of strange...

"When my mum and dad got divorced the first time, it was with Daddy Tommy. It was when I was six months old. And now they've got divorced again – my other daddy – Daddy Roger. So now it's been six months that my mum and Daddy Roger have been divorced."

The whole family is even harder to manage at a time like Christmas. Richie has to divide himself between spending time at home with his mother, being taken out on the town by Roger and visiting Tommy and his new wife Vicky with their two sons. Then, of course, there are three sets of grandparents, not forgetting one or two aunts and uncles.

His natural father, Daddy Tommy, married Carol when they were young and Tommy was a new recruit to the New York City Police Department. Richie was born about a year later, but there were soon difficulties between his mum and dad. They separated and Carol was left to bring up Richie on her own. But Tommy has always remained loyal to his only child. He has seen Richie every Saturday throughout his childhood and Carol says he has never missed a week, even after Roger arrived.

Carol got to know Roger quite soon after Tommy left and they married when Richie was four years old. Roger started life as a dock worker and has gradually pushed his way up to being Vice President of a trucking company. He is just as ambitious for Richie as he has been for himself.

"I want Richie to be a doctor or a lawyer or a dentist. In the beginning it was an obsession with me to the point where he would tell me he wanted to be a fireman or a policeman and I cannot accept that. That is too mediocre for me."

When Roger moved in, Richie was no different from any child expected to treat a near-stranger like a father. He could not really understand what was going on and felt resentful that Roger was suddenly between him and his mother. But in time Richie grew attached to Roger

DADDY ROGER: 'Richie is the only thing in my life that I'm proud of. He takes priority.'

DADDY TOMMY: 'We have an awful lot in common. Richie is competitive like me.'

and was happy to call him 'Daddy'. He started to feel that, although Tommy was his father, Roger was his Daddy, and somehow closer.

But Richie was not the only one who had to adjust. It was also tough for Tommy, having to share his son's affections with another man. At first, Roger was angry that Tommy would not allow him to adopt Richie and wanted to continue seeing him every week.

"In the beginning I felt it an affront," recalls Roger. "The way he found me to be the intruder. I felt Tommy to be the intruder. What wound up happening was I put Richie first. Tommy was his father and I could not deny him his father. As long as Tommy understood that the only thing I cared about was Richie, and as long as the only thing Tommy cared about was Richie, I had no problem."

It took nearly a year for Roger to accept that both he and Tommy could be fathers to Richie. Eventually things became reasonably harmonious, and Richie accepted that he had one father at home during the week and another to go out with at weekends. Then, when Richie was about nine years old, things started to go wrong between Carol and Roger and one day Roger packed a suitcase. Richie was used to seeing Daddy Roger set off on business trips but Roger remembers how Richie knew immediately that this was no normal departure.

"I walked downstairs with the suitcase and met Richie coming up. He looked at me and said: 'Daddy...Daddy, you're not going on a trip.' I went back upstairs, unpacked the suitcase and stayed six more months."

When Roger finally did leave, he and Carol tried to break it gently to Richie. They sat around the kitchen table and talked about the rows and explained that nothing would really change. But that did not make it any easier for Richie to accept.

"I was in the kitchen and my mum just told me – me and your dad are going to get separated. And I went, like 'eh?' It was: 'Why? Why are you getting separated.' They didn't seem to fight that much, so I didn't know why."

Richie felt betrayed but helpless. He was angry and he rebutted all Roger's attempts to make peace. For a while his only words to his second father were: 'You left me.' His school work suffered and he gave his mother a hard time.

"He got wilder at first because Roger was a very strict disciplinarian," says Carol. "But Roger spoke to him and said: 'Help mommy. You're the man of the house now, while I'm not here.' And he immediately took responsibility for that. He took over right away. 'Mommy, I'll help you do this – throw out the garbage and take in the mail and feed the cat.' He just took it on. He did it himself."

Now, six months after Roger moved out, Richie has accepted the situation, although he is still reluctant to talk very much about it. He has lost two fathers from everyday home life, but he has not lost their love. On the contrary he is now showered with affection, attention and treats as his mother and his two fathers each try to maintain their relationship with him and make sure he loves them. Being at the centre of three parents' attention makes Richie feel somehow responsible for them. He acts much older with them than he is. Carol says: "He's ten going on thirty."

Keeping each of Richie's relationships going takes some organising. His mum has to find a way of sharing him out equally three ways.

During the week he lives with Carol and he calls her house home, not Tommy's or Roger's.

Richie attends a local elementary school where he does well in most subjects and has a reputation for being a bit of a clown. His mother works full time and is rarely home before him. So Richie has a key to let himself in. Sometimes he waits at home on his own, watching cartoons on television while he does his homework. But two to three hours is a long time for a ten-year-old to be in the house alone. So most days he likes to go to his Grandma's house. They have an arrangement with a local taxi firm and all he has to do is call their number and they come and pick him up.

Richie is also a walking telephone directory. The phone is the only way he gets to talk with his two fathers during the week, so he has memorised each of their numbers, both at work and at home.

"Richie understands something," says Roger. "He has my New York number in memory. Whether I travel or I'm here in New York my company has one known fact. If he dials that phone and he wants me – I don't care where I am, anywhere in the United States – they will hold him on the line until they get to me, because my rule is – point blank – if he calls for me and you hang up in his face you don't have a job when I find out about it. It's that simple."

Richie spends the evenings at home with his mum, although she wishes she could see him for more than an hour or two and wants to change to part-time work. During the week they sort out the complex weekend arrangements and Richie's great memory for phone numbers comes in handy. Carol acts as go-between, negotiating when and where he'll be. The usual pattern is that Richie spends Saturdays with Daddy Tommy and Sundays with Daddy Roger. But now Saturdays don't feel quite the same to Richie any more. He has been used to having Daddy Tommy to himself, but Tommy has got married again and his new wife Vicky has two children already, Anthony, nine, and Tommy, five. "Vicky has two boys," says Richie, "and we usually play together because my Dad has to work on the house. So it's kind of strange because I used to play with my Dad, but now I don't. It's fun playing with Anthony, but we don't agree on a lot of things like normal brothers and sisters."

Daddy Tommy still feels close to Richie from these weekend visits. "We have an awful lot in common, Richie and I," he says. "Richie is competitive like I am. Sometimes it's good, sometimes it's bad, but he does love sports like I do – baseball, football or basketball. It makes it easy for me to take him out when I see him at weekends to games and stuff like that.

"I've stayed pretty well in touch, because even though Carol and I are divorced we're more or less, because of Richie, a brother and sister – just to make sure that Richie grows up the right way. We never argue or anything in front of him, and we just try to keep everything, you know, pretty good. Vicky's children are a little younger than Richie, but he ought to get acclimatised to having other children around. Being an only child, he has sometimes a little problem with not being the centre of attention, but everything's gone all right, pretty well so far.

"We do have some good times together, all the kids, because little Tommy, Vicky's son, and Anthony once in a while when they're all out playing ball, they forget their jealousy of each other and everything because, you know, they jockey for position – who's going to get the most attention sometimes – but when they're out there playing, it goes right out of their head and it makes us feel good too, you know, that we know that they can play together."

On Sundays Richie is collected by Roger, who enjoys taking him out to dinner in Manhattan and showing him the bright lights. They too are having to work out a new way of relating to

CAROL: 'Richie took over when Roger left...threw out the garbage and fed the cat.'
each other now that Roger is no longer involved in Richie's daily care.

"Richie is mine," says Roger. "I have raised him. I have put him in the tub when he had 104 fever. I have watched his birthdays one by one. Richie is the only thing in my life that I'm proud of, that I want nothing but the best for. He takes priority over all else."

The arrangements are practical and work out well for Roger, Tommy and Carol. Richie has a lot of power over the adults when it comes to the treats and outings they each give him; it is up for grabs who takes him ice-skating or bowling or to the latest film. And as for the question of where he'll spend Christmas, Richie is left wondering how he will divide his time between being at home with his mum, going out to Manhattan with Daddy Roger and spending time with the boys at Daddy Tommy's house. At least wherever he is he will not be short of the full attention of at least one of his three "parents" in his mixed-up, split-up world.

ELIZA: REFUGEE FROM WAR

'We saw our friends running away and we had to run too. At the border there was so much rain the vehicle could not move'

MOZAMBIQUE
ZAMBIA

ELIZA was helping her mother in the maize plantation when the rebels came.

For some weeks past she had heard her father talking nervously with the other village men about "Tchanga". Tchanga is the local word for the Renamo guerillas, a part-political, part-bandit group secretly finance by South Africa to destabilise the socialist government of Mozambique. They had been ravaging the north of the country for ten years and now the men had heard of attacks on nearby villages.

None of the talk had meant much to Eliza. She had not known what it was to meet Tchanga. Now she knew.

She knew from the look of fear in her mother's eyes and the shouts and cries of the children. Tchanga means an end of everything a child in a remote village has ever known; an end to playing in the plantation and around the few straw-thatched huts and trees that she knew so well. Tchanga means running away with your family and leaving everything behind, running for day after endless day through unfamiliar lands. Tchanga means destruction, burning and death.

Asked to talk about what happened, Eliza can offer only a blur of confused impressions of those savage times. She remembers travelling by foot and cart or truck; she remembers hostile and friendly people and places as the fear of Tchanga drove her family further and further away from home and closer to

STARTING AGAIN: Eliza in her new home.

UKWIMI CAMP: *Eliza's family got a blanket each, cooking pots, a hoe, grain and beans.*

the Zambian border where they were eventually picked up by Zambian officials working with the United Nations High Commission for Refugees.

"We saw our friends running away and we had to run too. We got to the border and started to cultivate a field. Then the officials stopped us and a vehicle came to pick us up. It dropped us at Vubu. At Vubu we...we spent one night and then we were dropped at Chipata. At Chipata we spent several days. There was much rain – so much water on the road that the vehicle could not move. We travelled by vehicle coming here."

"Here" is a long line of tents, known as the Ukwimi Refugee Settlement in Zambia's South Eastern Province. It is the end of Eliza's journey, at least for the time being. But it is not the end of her problems.

It is dark by the time she and her exhausted family reach the settlement. All have survived the terrible experience – her father and mother, her grandmother, two sisters and the baby snuggled up against her mother's breast. But one look at Eliza's face tells just how strained, tired and battered they all are.

The man in charge tells them: "Because the sun has gone you will get your provisions tomorrow."

So next morning Eliza's family queue like military recruits in the early morning light to receive their official provisions: one blanket per person, one set of cooking pots, one hoe and one week's supply of grains and beans. The bare necessities and very welcome, but not much to start building a new future with.

Ukwimi had been set up less than nine months before Eliza's family arrived. Several thousand hectares have been set aside ready to absorb more and more families fleeing from the war. There are already two thousand children in the camp and they outnumber the adults by nearly two to one. The war has taken away so many parents and grandparents.

The family soon settle into their new life, establishing order and routines. The children help with the work, pounding the maize, collecting the water and looking after the young ones.

It is a strange new life in a strange new place. These are people whose lifestyle revolves around cultivating a dusty patch of land and grazing their cattle. That land is far behind and they are never likely to return to it. The cattle are gone too. Even if they could have brought them, the cattle would not have been allowed into Ukwimi. This is tsetse fly country and cattle are forbidden until the government's eradication programme is complete.

Now the Zambian government is looking ahead for constructive ways to cope with the increasing numbers of refugees pouring into their country.

Within a few weeks Eliza and her family will be allotted their own plot of land. Here they can begin to clear the ground for cultivation and build a round, straw-thatched hut, just like the one they left behind so far away in Mozambique – so long ago it seems, before an innocent girl who has seen too much, been through too much, learned what it was to know Tchanga.

FRIDAY: NIGHTMARE OF WAR

'They chopped my father with an axe and stabbed my mother and the baby. I dream about it and it makes me cry very much'

ZAMBIA

'THE Tchangas came to our village. They chased us and caught us. They took all our things away – cattle, chickens, the bicycle, everything. Houses were burnt, everything was set on fire, including the maize. They even made us undress, took our clothes and burned them.

Then...they started on my father. They tied him to a tree and chopped with an axe. They left him...dead. Then they grabbed my mother and did bad things to her. Afterwards they tied her up and stabbed her...they cut her up. My baby sister was still on my mother's back. Then they killed her with the very knife they'd killed my mother. They stabbed the baby on the back.

I ran into the bush and managed to escape, I found my sister and her husband who lived in another place. They looked after me. But the Tchangas came again, and we all ran away. We walked and walked until at last we found ourselves here in Zambia.

Now I am safe. I have enough food to eat, and I have some clothes to wear. But I can't forget how my mother was killed. Sometimes I dream about it. It is always the same kind of dream. Sometimes it makes me cry very much. I wake up in the night feeling frightened, or I cry when I think about my dream in the morning.

In one dream the enemy soldiers came and picked me up and threw me on the fire. Then my mother came to me. She talked to me and said: 'Wake up!'

But the soldiers asked her what she was doing and stabbed her until she was dead. Then I woke up, still in my dream, heard gun shots and tried to jump into the water. After a while, when I saw that they had gone, I came out of the water and ran away and found myself in Zambia.

Now I am still with my sister, and I cultivate a small field to get food. But I want to do well at school, because one day I would like to be a teacher.'

ALONE: 'In one dream the enemy soldiers picked me up and threw me on the fire.'

PARAMESHWAR: THE MIGRANT

'I don't like Bombay. It's nothing like the village where I came from. There are no birds, just a building site. When I grow up, I would like to go back'

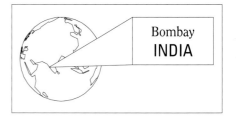

PARAMESHWAR'S family is one of thousands attracted to the city to work on the building sites as bonded labour. Their children are exposed to many health hazards and there are numerous accidents. Parameshwar is fortunate that the Mobile Creche movement have succeeded in negotiating to establish a school and nursery for the workers' children, one of 16 such projects so far.

‘My name is Parameshwar. I'm the oldest in our family – ten years old. I have a younger brother and two sisters. We all live in a tent on a building site in Bombay. My parents came here when I was a baby. They used to live in a village a long way away in the country. But there was no money in the village, no work. They had to come here to earn money.

My mother works as a labourer, carrying soil in a scoop balanced on her head. She used to carry bricks, but she's been ill and they are too heavy for her now. My father works in the quarry breaking the rocks for building. But he's not well either. He has bad boils on his body.

BIG CITY: 'In the village there were sheep, cattle, tomatoes and a river. I don't like it here.'

When my parents can work, they're given money by the foreman. Then they can buy enough food for us to have a cooked meal every day. Each morning my job is to collect the water. We have five large cans that I must take to the tap and fill whenever they are empty.

I used to work carrying water and washing glasses for one of the tea-shops on the site. I could earn about fifty rupees a month *{about two pounds}*. But one day I felt unwell. I tried to lift the buckets of water but couldn't. So I went home and slept so deeply I couldn't open my eyes. I had to go to the hospital for medicines. I didn't go back to that job.

Now there is a Mobile Creche on the building site, I go there with my brother and sisters. My little sister plays and my brother draws pictures or makes a building with wooden blocks. I cut nails for the small children in the nursery, but sometimes I have to stay at home to stand guard over our tent.

CARE: 'I help small children in the nursery.'

I haven't always lived here. When I was six my mother sent me back to her home village, called Telgaon. It took many hours to get there on trains and a bus. I lived with my aunt and worked with my uncle and grandfather on the farm. We used to grow tomatoes, chillies, tamarind fruit, beans, everything. We used to take the sheep out for grazing and the cattle. At midday we used to bring the cattle back, tie them and milk them. Then we'd have lunch and a sleep. There wasn't any firewood so my job was to get some. There was a river and I used to take the boat to collect sacks of fuel to bring back to the village. I liked everything about that village. But the school there was no good, so I had to come back to live with my parents here in Bombay.

I don't like this place. I don't like living here. It's nothing like the village where I came from. When I arrived there wasn't a sparrow here. There were no birds, not a soul. Just a building under construction. When I grow up I'd like to go back to Telgaon.

JIMMY AND BIDDY: TRAVELLERS

'I'll tell you why caravans are better than houses. The rats are outside a caravan, but they're inside a house'

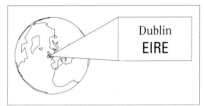

Dublin
EIRE

JIMMY: 'I got in a fight. I got hurt, but so did he.'

'MY NAME is Jimmy and I'm eight. My sister Ellen is ten. Biddy is five and Debbie is three. Then there's my brother Mickey, who's three. We live in a trailer on a site outside Dublin. We live in a trailer because we don't like living in houses. You see, country people are richer than travelling people. They live in houses. We don't.

We lived in a house once. I thought it was good, but only for a few days. There was trouble with the people. I didn't like 'em. One day I was going over the shop on my bike and a young fellow pissed on me. I went up home and told me mammy. She went down their house.

They used to call us names and stuff at school, like 'Nackers' and 'Bowsies'. That was when they didn't clout us. I got in a fight once. Small fellow, right. Called he would kill me and all this. He started a fight. I got hurt, but so did he.'

PAGE 66

I'M BIDDY. I'll tell you why it wasn't very nice when we lived in the house. There was a load of rats there. When my mammy shook the crumbs off my dress, they were thrown on the carpet and a load of rats came out big. Rats came along the carpet and ate them. Daddy catched two of them. That's why we never lived in a house any more. Daddy decided to go in the caravan. I feel more better here, because the rats are outside a caravan, not inside. A house is bigger than a caravan. If you wanted to climb up on a house you'd have to get a big, big ladder, wouldn't you. If you wanted to climb up a trailer you'd only have to get a small ladder.

In the dark time, if it gets real, real, real dark, the rats come out. Probably there's some up on

BIDDY (left): 'In the big trailer there's spiders. The small trailer's lovely.'

the wall or hiding in the ditch. Rats. In the ditch. I saw two yesterday at dark time. When Daddy asked me to hold a rat by the tail, I wouldn't. But I think he and Jimmy threw them out in the garden. The dog was eating them. I can draw a picture of them for you. When we lived in a real house, I used to water the plants. I had a watering can, right. I went upstairs. I was hiding, right, and I got water in it and I spilled water all over the cats.

There's all spiders, you know, in the big trailer. There's all spiders and there's little midges and all. There's big flies, well two flies anyway, big flies, all flies. But the inside of the small trailer is lovely. Not like the big trailer. In the small trailer you can make a bed out of bunks. You lift up the table and chairs. I know how to make mammy's bed. It's easy. But I don't know how to make Jimmy's bed. Mammy puts us to bed. You know, when I woke up in the night there was a candle light. I couldn't see the candle, but when I got up on Mammy's bed I blowed it out – with my fingers.

CHRISTINA: ORPHANAGE GIRL

'I am very, very happy here. They have a waterfall and toys and parties, and we only get hit when necessary'

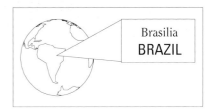

Brasilia
BRAZIL

CHRISTINA'S home life ended the day her mother killed her father. In the slums of Brasilia her mother could not cope, her father drank and was hardly ever around and Christina shared her misery with five brothers.

"My mother sent my father to buy meat," remembers Christina. "But he didn't buy any. Instead he bought pingo and got drunk. When he arrived home he was so drunk he threatened to kill my mother with a knife. My mother threw boiling water on him and then threw him down the well."

Suddenly her father was dead, her mother on the run from the police, and six-year-old Christina was one of 60 children at the Lar Betel orphanage. Every child there has a story to tell – a story of deprivation, ill-treatment or abandonment. The orphanage is a shambling, crumbling building, that only a few years before was an overcrowded nightmare of a refuge for children. Then Pastor Enrico and his wife Josephine took it over and transformed it into a secure and loving home.

Christina was very frightened when she arrived at Lar Betel and hardly spoke at all. Her five brothers were taken to the orphanage with her. The oldest was twelve and deeply disturbed. He soon ran away to join thousands of other street children in the capital and has never been seen or heard from since. The second brother, Joao Batista, stayed. But he too wore the scars of distress. He was small and thin, drawn and emaciated with bad sores on his legs. The other children gave him the nickname Mosquitino. He was always shivering and always hugging himself as if cold.

The three other brothers were younger than Christina. There was Daniel, five, Marcelo, four, and J.S., only three and very confused by the sudden wrench from his mother. They needed a lot of attention, which is in short supply in an orphanage. But even at six years old Christina was used to being expected to look after the little ones and her feelings of responsibility helped her to adjust to her new life. She did her best to dress, feed and comfort them, and the staff called her 'The Little Mother'. At the same time she began to thrive physically, losing the look of fear in her eyes and some of her shy reserve. But she also found time to play with her two precious plastic dolls with their permed blonde hair. Everyone knew which was Christina's bed in the tightly-packed dormitory because her dolls were always propped up at the end of it along with her cuddly blue rabbit with its long ears and frilly dress. She always arranged them the same way, in exactly the same places.

As the months went by Christina became more and more settled. She started to make progress at school and run around with the other children in the yard. But the city orphanage only takes babies and young children. Once Christina was seven she had to move on. Her fragile security was under threat for the second time in less than a year.

Christina's prospects were not so grim as they seemed. Pastor Enrico dreamed when he took over the orphanage of a better home for children like Christina, away from the hopelessness of

SKILL: 'I've learnt to crochet. I make little bootees, little sandals and dolls' clothes.'

the city slums. The dream became real when the orphanage was given a stretch of farmland 70 miles out in the country. There were no buildings, no proper road and there had been no previous cultivation. It would be a challenge for anyone, but especially for a bunch of kids, many quite young and some retarded or disturbed. But the farm project went ahead and all the children from seven to eighteen were brought out from the orphanage. They called it the Fazenda Betel and within five years it was a thriving, almost self-sufficient farm and home for 140 boys and girls.

And so the day came for Christina to pack up her things and leave the city orphanage. But that meant saying goodbye to her two smallest brothers, Marcelo and J.S. The 'Little Mother' had no choice but to leave them behind. Only six-year-old Daniel was allowed to go with her, a year earlier than he should, so she would not be moved completely on her own. Christina was given a plastic carrier-bag to put her things in and went into the dormitory for the last time. Firstly, she laid her dolls carefully at the bottom of the bag. Then she went over to her cubbyhole and took her spare dress and T-shirt and her toothbrush. Few other children would be able to pack up all their possessions quite so quickly.

When the ancient truck arrived, all the children were out in the yard to see their friends off. Christina handed her plastic bag to the driver and turned to hug Marcelo and J.S. for the last time until they finally come to join her in the country. That would be in around two years, but to Christina and her brothers it seemed like a lifetime away. They were ready to go. But at the last moment Christina could not resist running back to hug the little ones just one more time.

Then she was off – off to change from being the eldest in the orphanage to being the youngest at the farm. As the hard grey lines of concrete apartment blocks gave way to the gentler green of the Brazilian countryside, she pulled open the top of her crackly plastic bag and peered down into the darkness, just checking her precious dolls. Then with a show of almost unbelievable courage, Christina even started to enjoy the longest journey she and Daniel had ever made, singing loudly all the way. Finally they turned onto a rutted dirt track and bumped their way the last few miles to Fazenda Betel. That track has a reputation for shortening the useful life of the ancient farm vehicles by several years.

Shouts rang out across the farm as soon as the old truck came into view. Christina's arrival was as big an event for the farm children as her farewell had been for the little ones back in Brasilia. Everybody dropped tools to come to greet them, headed by the flamboyant figure of Pastor Enrico, complete with cowboy hat. Christina and Daniel already knew him well from his weekly visits to the city orphanage. The children's affection for him as their only father-figure is enormous, even if they do have to share his warm embraces with nearly 200 others.

As the welcoming party went back to work, Christina was taken off to find where she will sleep. There are just two long dormitory buildings on the farm, each divided into large rooms, supervised by one of the older children. Christina was allocated one of the bottom bunks packed end-to-end along each side wall.

She immediately began to lay out her things with the same methodical care that she packed them six hours before. Once again her treasured dolls were first. She tenderly arranged their hair and propped them side by side at the head of her bed.

Meanwhile, Daniel had been reunited with his brother, Mosquitino, who had already been at the farm for several months. It was quite a reunion for the boys and it brought out all Mosquitino's old insecurities, uncontrollably slapping his hands around himself in nervous, hugging gestures. All that day Mosquitino clung anxiously on to his little brother's hands as much for his own security as in a sign of welcome.

Soon it was time for Christina and Daniel to join the other children in the dining-area. It was still only partly-built with half a roof, so when it rained all the children had to squash up one end. There was no electricity, so all the cooking was done on a woodstove which the children had to keep feeding with dry wood. Christina was used to eating in large groups of noisy children, but she had always been one of the biggest ones. Now she looked and felt tiny as she lifted her huge tray up to the adult-sized counter to be loaded with rice, beans, green peppers and meat.

Christina soon settled into the secure rhythm of an outdoor life where children are expected to take full responsibility for themselves and the farm.

"When I wake up I comb my hair, clean my cupboard and make my bed," she says. "Then I get dressed and clean my teeth. I get a cup and have my breakfast and then I clean my teeth again. In the morning I clean the yard, in the afternoon I clean the bathroom and in the evening I clean my bedroom. I work too and I go to school. We have things like mathematics, science and Portuguese. We only get hit when necessary, when we disobey. Then there's play time."

Christina enjoyed the routine and soon became part of the community. A year later, she is a different child from the frightened, withdrawn girl who first went to the orphanage. In fact the little girl who would hardly speak has turned into a chatterbox.

"I am very, very happy here. When I arrived I liked it a lot. There were so many good things. What I liked the best was the waterfall and the kitchen garden. I love the stories of the three pigs and Red Riding Hood and everything here. Here they don't hit you very much and they have toys and parties. Christmas was very good. I got a lot of things. I got dolls that I dress and toys

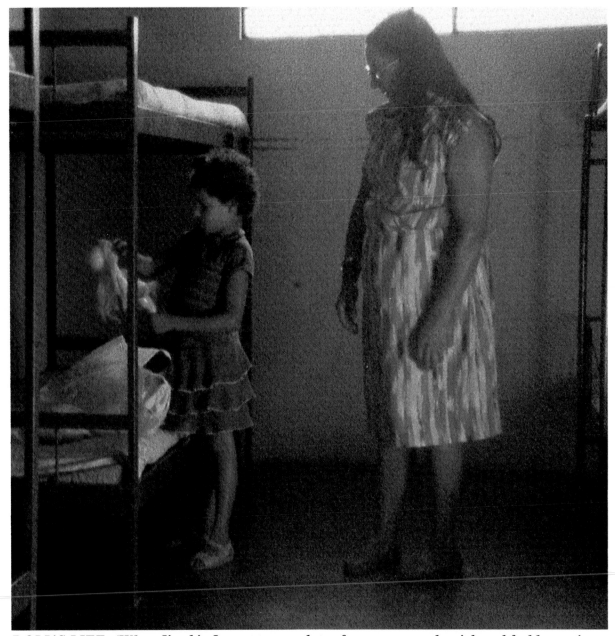

DOLL'S LIFE: 'When I'm big I want to earn lots of money, cure the sick and feel happy.'

and clothes and something to tie my hair up with. Christmas for me was a feast, and was all about the birth of Jesus. There was a play and lots of games and two feasts."

Christina has learned to work alongside the other children on the farm, as they tend the chickens, feed the pigs, milk the cows and ride the horses like regular gauchos. As time goes on she will be taught how to cultivate a wide range of crops, including rice, maize, beans, mangoes, oranges and papayas.

The only part of farm life that Christina has found hard to get used to is the poisonous snakes that are everywhere. There are as many snakes as children. Pastor Enrico keeps a display of bottled snakes outside the small dispensary he runs for sick children. Many of the children consider snake a delicacy and they had shared a 1·2 metre boa on the day before Christina arrived. Some of the older girls have been teaching Christina to crochet little things, including dolls' clothes.

"I've learnt to crochet, more or less," she says excitedly. "I haven't learnt to do covers, but I already know how to make little bootees, little sandals, and dolls' clothes, and knickers for dolls. I know how to make lots of things."

The farm, like the city orphanage, is supported by a religious charity. All the children are expected to take part in the daily hymn-singing and prayers. Christina joins in with complete conviction.

"I thank God with all my heart;

I thank God for sharing and all we have in common;

I thank God because he gave me real peace;

I thank God that he delivered me from all wrong and let me live."

The Fazenda Betel is not a solution to all the children's problems. Many are still disturbed during the day and have trouble sleeping at nights. Sometimes older children drop out and head back to the attractions of the city. Drugs are always a danger, especially among children referred by the courts after years on the streets. One group of boys, deprived of their drugs, made up a smoking mixture by combining toothpaste with the filling from their mattresses. Pastor Enrico found out what was going on, but not before the corners had been torn from many mattresses. The boys, and the mattresses, are still there.

Christina has not lost all contact with her mother, who has married again. Christina even went to spend a few days with her. She was excited and expected a lot, but things did not work out and for a while she became withdrawn again and was happy to return to the farm.

She is not the youngest any more and is starting to take responsibility for others. The farm has given Christina a lot, but perhaps the greatest gift of all has been hope. She has even started talking about the future, because now, at last, she feels that she has a future.

"When I'm big," she says proudly, "I want to be a sailor. Or I want to work as a driver, be a worker, do lots of things. I want to be an employee and earn lots of money. I want to buy clothes and shoes and lots of things. When I was small and even before I was born I wanted to be a magic person who could cure others who were sick. I want to have the gift of curing. I want to feel very happy."

CHAPTER FOUR: WORK

MELINDA: ON THE SCRAP HEAP

'If I collect a lot of rubbish I can sell it for about 25p. We're always hoping that one day we'll find a goldmine'

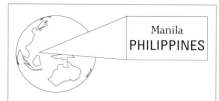

Manila
PHILIPPINES

THEY call it Smokey Mountain. A 70ft high pile of rotting, stinking, smouldering, poisonous, jagged rubbish that spreads over more than thirty festering acres above Manila in the Philippines. On rubbish dumps like this the world over, flocks of hungry gulls can be seen searching for scraps. The only difference here on Smokey Mountain is that the birds don't get a look in. The hordes of scavengers are people, and many of them children.

Children like 11-year-old Melinda who spends up to twelve hours a day on its hideous slopes. Her goal is to pick through the filth under the wheels of giant bulldozers to find a bottle top here, a bit of plastic there, maybe a sliver of metal.

If she's lucky in those twelve hours, she'll find enough to sell to the scrapmen for about 25p and her family will be able to eat that night. Melinda lives with her

MELINDA: Scavenging for a few pence a day.

parents and two younger sisters in one of the shanty settlements that litter the foothills. Even her crude lean-to shack is built on top of rubbish and largely made of rubbish – rusty iron sheets, tattered bits of plastic, old cartons and sheets of plywood. But in huts like this Smokey Mountain houses 20,000 people, 9,000 of them children, and all of them hungry.

Every day Melinda wakes to the throbbing roar of a massive bulldozer starting up. Her mother helps tie an old vest around her head as some protection against the flies that swarm everywhere. Then Melinda picks her way through the maze of shacks, wades though a stinking, mosquito-infested lake and begins the slow climb up to the top. She doesn't seem to notice the sweet, sickly smell that makes any outsider retch. She isn't even alarmed when her feet hit a soft patch and she begins to sink into the filth. Once at the top she joins the other scavengers – girls, boys, mothers and fathers – flocking around the bulldozer, dodging past the great steel blade as it cuts into the garbage, swooping in close to the bone-crushing wheels, searching for a choice morsel. Melinda knows that the best pickings are to be found in the most dangerous place of all,

SEARCH: 'I'm looking for bottles, metal, pigs' bones, toothpaste tubes and plastic.'

DREAM: 'We always hope that one day we'll find a goldmine here. I haven't found much.'

HOPE: 'I want to help my father so that we can have a meal every day.'

right under the wheels of the bulldozers when they have just been fed a new truck-load fresh from the Manila suburbs. The most reckless children have even been known to climb on to the backs of trucks as they arrive, tumbling out with the load as the truck tips. With her old shopping basket in one hand and a sharp spiked steel rod called a 'kalahig' in the other, Melinda is soon at work among the rotting refuse.

Melinda knows exactly what she's looking for and exactly what it's worth. "What I'm looking for are bottles, aluminium, metal, bones from pigs, the crown from the soft-drinks seal, tubes of toothpaste, plastics. When I've collected things I put them in my basket. Then I keep on searching until 5 o'clock in the evening until it's time to go down to the junk shop."

She concentrates fiercely on her work. There's little conversation among the scavengers – the competition is intense and there are frequent squabbles. Even when they want to talk their voices are lost under the roar of the bulldozers that loom through the smoke like tanks on a battlefield.

The truth is, there isn't a great deal to be found among the refuse of Manila life, especially not when you are picking over rubbish that has already been worked over by hundreds of others, all equally desperate. If only Melinda could scavenge on the virgin garbage tips in Europe or North America. Even half an hour sorting through the average dustbin would yield a fortune to her – far more than she could hope to glean from days on Smokey Mountain. But like all desperate people, Melinda survives on hope and the stories of treasures that she might discover.

"We're always hoping that one day we'll find a goldmine here. I haven't found any valuable things here among all the rubbish yet. But I have a friend whose name is Melvin and he has found a pair of earrings, a necklace, a wrist-watch, money, a ring, things like that."

The dream of finding something valuable...one day...some day...keeps Melinda going. But she is always glad when it is time to sling her bag over her shoulder and head back down the mountain to the dealers. There she tips her bag out on the floor and sorts out her collection, metal in one pile, bottles in another, plastic in another, and so on. Everything is weighed by the dealers. They are the powerful ones, fixing the prices that spell the difference between a decent daily meal or none at all for children like Melinda. They often employ their own gangs of scavengers to work day and night. Not a word is spoken until Melinda has been told how much she has earned.

"If I have collected a lot of rubbish, I can sell it for eight pesos {about 25 pence}. But if there's not much to collect, I only earn six pesos a day {about 18 pence}."

And while Melinda works at the top of the mountain, down below her younger sisters are out to play. Their playground is a pile of junk, too. There they poke about like apprentices to their sister's craft, unearthing whatever dangerous playthings take their fancy. Fun for them is shuffling through piles of waste paper like other children play in the autumn leaves on a woodland floor. When the wind blows, as it frequently does, all the tattered paper and torn plastic is whipped up into the air to rain back down on their heads and their homes. For the smallest ones the piles of rotten fruit, stale bread and vegetables that their parents sort out to feed their pigs are often too much to resist. Gastro-enteritis, worms and dysentery follow, fuelling the already-high infant mortality rates.

Smokey Mountain has been a scandal in the Philippines for more than thirty years, ever since the first garbage was dumped on the site of what was once the sleepy fishing village of Barrio

Magdaragat. In 1983 the Marcos regime tore down the scavengers' shanty dwellings and tried to entice them to a new settlement with proper sanitation. But families cannot live on clean water alone and the scavengers soon drifted back to the only security they knew – the security of the rubbish dump. Today there are more positive projects, such as those run by the Institute For The Protection Of Children, with a health clinic, a four-room school on the very top of the rubbish tip, and even a new Parish Of The Risen Christ at Smokey Mountain. And in 1988 President Aquino's government finally started to look actively for ways in which low cost housing and industrial development could offer the next generation a better future than scavenging.

But it may be too late for Melinda. She has already taken her place as one of the youngest full-time recruits to a life on the scrap heap.

Melinda has survived early childhood, but her health is just as much at risk scrambling around all day in a concentrated breeding ground of infection and noxious fumes. Tuberculosis and other respiratory conditions are a major hazard to the Smokey Mountain scavengers. Her mother does what she can to protect Melinda from the dirt and disease. She has found her a pair of old Wellington boots, which is a great deal better than many children who have nothing but a pair of flip-flops. When Melinda comes home at the end of the day her mother helps her off with her working clothes and washes her from head to toe. They have no bath or shower, and even drinking water has to be bought at Smokey Mountain. But there is a communal tap which provides salty water that serves for washing. Every evening Melinda's mother pours a plastic bucket of water over her daughter and then methodically soaps every part of her head and body. She is glad to see her daughter back in clean clothes and heading off down the long garbage-strewn alley that leads off Smokey Mountain and into the main street.

Like most eleven-year-olds, Melinda loves to get out and meet up with her friends. She is one of the big girls and a natural leader. Melinda is the one who gets the games started, chalks out the six-squared pitch, picks the teams and generally bosses her younger friends about. They don't seem to mind, because Melinda also has a wicked sense of humour and soon has them all laughing.

Melinda's mother regrets that her daughter's childhood has turned out this way and worries that she will soon face many new dangers and temptations. Solvent abuse is a widespread problem among Smokey Mountain teenagers looking for an easy escape from a bleak present and an equally bleak future. Teenage suicide is not uncommon. Many young girls drift into the city in search of excitement. What they usually find instead is destitution from which they can only find a way out through prostitution. Melinda's mother's hopes are based on faith rather than her own ability to help.

"I hope she will meet a good man when the time comes. It would be nice if he were to be rich, but best of all if he is a good man. I hope with the help of Our Lord and His Blessed Mother that she will have an easier life than me, but I've got a good man and a family and I thank God for them."

Melinda's parents care deeply about her welfare. They know that her health is at risk on Smokey Mountain. So why do they live there? Because they don't feel there is any other choice. Like most families in the crowded settlements they came from the provinces where they used to work on the plantations. But without land or regular employment, they drifted to the city in the vain hope of finding work. Smokey Mountain is one step up from the alternative – sleeping on

BATH: Mum says: 'I hope she will meet a good man. It would be nice if he were rich.'

PLAY: *Melinda is a natural leader and soon has all the other children laughing.*

the streets. At least they have a roof and a shack and can make some sort of living, however meagre. Melinda's mother says: "Her father and I are both illiterate; so we have no choice but to stay here. We're better off than those with no homes who have to live on the streets."

Without even a rudimentary education, Melinda has little chance of escaping from this poverty. But her mother did not force her to give up school at such an early age. That was Melinda's own brave decision, and Melinda's alone. She knows how desperate is the life she has been born into and by the age of ten she understood the reality that faced her family. She recognised the downcast expression on her father's face at the end of an unproductive day when there was not enough food to go around. And she decided to do something about it.

"I left school because I want to help my father so that we can have a meal every day, my sisters and me. If I didn't help him, we might not be able to afford to eat at all."

EDISON, CAYO & JOSE-ROBERTO: SHOE-SHINE BOYS

'I don't smoke drugs any more, not now, I've pulled myself together. I still smoke just once in a while'

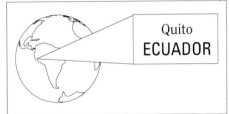

Quito **ECUADOR**

YOU can tell their trade by the skin on their hands. It is deeply stained with black wax, just like the ingrained soot that marked out the boy sweeps of Victorian London. Edison, Cayo and Jose-Roberto are shoe-shine boys.

To the men whose shoes they clean there is nothing to choose between them. Each carries a scruffy box full of waxes, cloths and brushes. Each kneels down over his footstand as he works. If a boy does a good job, they toss him a coin. If not – well, the boys soon learn to be on their guard. They know their place. Dispensable. Three among thousands who tout for trade along the streets of Quito, the capital city of Ecuador.

They spend far more time searching for customers than polishing shoes, their calls rising above the traffic, mingling with all the other girls and boys with something to sell: matches, cigarettes, sweets and, when times are tough, even their own bodies.

On the streets of other cities in the world – in London, Moscow, Washington or Tokyo – there is hardly a child to be seen alone. Quito's street-children should not be here, either. They are meant to be in school. But the lure of earning a few coins in the big city is too powerful. Often it is also the only way to make sure of getting a meal. Nobody knows just how many street-children there are all over the world. The best estimate is probably 30 million.

In Quito, the problem is acute. Streams of children flow down into the city, deep in an Andean basin, just like the rainfall running off the mountains.

Edison has been living on the street long enough to know all its vices – drugs, crime, prostitution and pimping. He will talk about his life only when he is high on dope or glue. But that makes it harder for him to be coherent – or honest.

"There was trouble...I had to leave my home...I was peeling potatoes when they came...I had a knife in my hand. Someone had stolen a tape-recorder and some money. So they accused me. They said they were going to put me in jail. So I jumped out of the highest window...I still had the knife in my hand. I hid until a man said if he saw me there again he'd arrest me.

"I came to Quito...I was sleeping in a doorway...I had all my money stolen...then I met up with my three friends...three brothers. They took me to sleep at their mother's house. They were poor but they gave me food."

It wasn't many weeks before Edison had his first experience of drugs.

"I was cleaning shoes one day when a gringo from Miami came and gave me a box and told me to 'have a go with this'. We called him Tin-Tin. I didn't know anything about drugs. I said: 'I don't know how' and he showed me what to do. You put the stuff in a can and sniff it up your nose. You end up sort of half-stoned." Edison has been half-stoned much of the time since. He found his way to the Sotano, one of several sanctuaries for Quito's street children; a refuge where up to seventeen boys can get a simple meal, some good advice and a place to sleep that is safer than the gutter. It is run in the basement of a theological college and staffed by young student volunteers under the supervision of Salesian priests. The Salesians do not try to stop the boys from working. In fact, they encourage them to earn a living in whatever honest way they can – shining shoes, selling newspapers, working in the market. If they can pay their way in the Sotano, so much the better. They are expected to hand over part of their earnings and in the process learn to calculate and budget. The young priests even help the boys make their own shoe-shine boxes.

EDISON: 'I want to learn mechanics.'

The Sotano workers know how hard it is to turn around boys like Edison. Before he arrived, drug-taking had already set in motion the familiar cycle of crime and degradation.

"Once I got caught and the police took my powder. Another time when the police tried to catch me I had a gold watch, a gold chain, a ring and a calculator. I was on the streets trying to sell them. I was with the three brothers. They ran one way and I ran another. But I fell and one of the police caught me. They beat me up badly.

"I was in prison for three months. I wanted to get out of there. It was horrible. Before they let me out, they ordered me to be beaten again."

The Sotano brought some rare stability to Edison's turbulent life while he was willing to go along with the authority of the priests.

The Padre responsible for the Sotano explained what he expects of the boys: "First, they must strive to become part of a community with the other boys. They must forget their vices, for instance stealing, lying, getting drunk and fighting. Next, we demand obedience to the Salesians who work with them. They must work, not spend the day lazing around. Each afternoon we expect them to hand over some of their earnings. Finally we look towards seeing some change in them, that they are leaving their vices behind and helping the other boys in the group. If they co-operate then they get the chance to go to San Patricio."

San Patricio is a training centre run by the priests out in the countryside. If the boys behave, they are sent there to learn a trade.

At first, Edison liked the Sotano – the fun and singing, football in the yard, helping to cook the simple evening meals and even learning to say Grace before eating. Edison recognised the opportunities the Sotano could open up and accepted the security of the nearest thing he had

CAYO: 'One day I hope I'll get qualifications. I'm learning to write and do sums.'

ever known to a caring home. He said: "If I do well here for three months, they'll send me to San Patricio to learn mechanics or carpentry. Otherwise I'll have to leave. I'll have to go back to living on the streets."

Two months later, that is exactly what happened. Edison was on the streets again, offering his own version of the reasons why.

"I had to leave. It was because I stole a shoe-shine box with two friends. The Salesian said I had to return the box. I didn't want to return it, so he took away my box too. I couldn't earn any money, but the Padre still asked me to hand over my savings at the end of the week, even though I didn't have my box. I said: 'No'. Then the Padre asked me if I had said my prayers and I said I hadn't. I was rude to him, so he sent me away."

Once again Edison was wandering down the back alleys of central Quito, mingling with petty criminals, drug-peddlers and pimps. His bed was a stretch of pavement near the bus station, huddled together with the other destitute children for warmth. The only difference was that now he didn't even have the means to earn his next meal – a shoe-shine box.

Edison drifted for more than six weeks before he was taken in by another refuge for street children at Mi Caleta. He claims to have given up drugs – well almost – and hopes to be

CHEEKY: There are as many as 30 million street kids in the world.

URCHINS: Thousands tout for trade along the streets of Quito in Ecuador.

accepted back at the Sotano, and eventually to learn a trade. "A month and a half ago they took me in at Mi Caleta. There I have a home. Now I can get a job, shining shoes and selling newspapers. Then I'll go to the Sotano and see if they'll take me there. The father said they could take me...and then I'll go to San Patricio to learn carpentry.

"I don't smoke drugs any more, not now. When I left my home I did a lot, but now I've almost forgotten about it. I've pulled myself together and got myself sorted out. I still smoke just a little, once in a while..."

Not all of the shoe-shine boys live on the streets. Some, like Cayo, even live at home with their parents. Every morning he and his mother leave home and walk down to La Merced Square.

"La Merced is a small market square," says Cayo. "There are stalls selling things. I help my mother get her stall set up to sell shoelaces, needles, buttons, combs. She buys them in the big stores in San Francisco Square and then re-sells them. I clean shoes in the square."

Because there are almost as many shoe-shine boys as there are customers with shoes to shine, Cayo must get down to the market early to get a good pitch. But he also has to watch out for the law.

"I've never had trouble with the police but other boys have," he says. "One time my brother – he should have had a permit – he was arguing with a policeman and hit him. He ended up in prison."

Cayo doesn't intend to spend many more years shining shoes. Although he has left school, he still wants to get at least some education.

"After we have finished at the market, we go back up to the house. I get my books and go to evening school, which starts at 7 o'clock. I play with my friends until the bell rings for my grade. Then we go inside and the teacher tells us that we're badly behaved, that we mustn't eat or talk in class. They teach me to write, add up, multiply, divide. They educate me there and then we have our homework to teach us multiplication and division. One day I hope I'll get some good qualifications. School finishes at about 9.45 in the evening. I have to queue for a bus home at night, by which time it's 10.30 and I'm ready for bed."

Another shoe-shine boy, Jose-Roberto, came to the Sotano at about the same time as Edison, but his future is more hopeful.

"I used to live with my father. He was a teacher. I used to go to his school. I was in Class 1. We had a good time together. But he was quite old. Then he died of a heart attack. I didn't have anywhere to live. I haven't got a mother. I haven't got any relatives. I only had my father – may he rest in peace.

"I didn't know what to do. I went to the Guayaquil bus terminus. A man told me to get on a bus to Quito. He said I might find work here. I said OK. I was tired and fell asleep for the whole journey. I didn't wake up until the next morning when we arrived in the Quito bus terminus. At first I didn't know where I was. I thought I was still at the Guayaquil bus terminus.

"I wandered around the city trying to find someone who would give me work. I went from house to house. The worst thing was not having anything to eat. I got very tired and very weak. Eventually I found work in a restaurant. I worked there for nearly three months. Then I went to another job in a carpenter's workshop. That was another three months. Then there were other jobs, some for just a few weeks. Eventually I met a boy called Felipe. He told me to go to a woman's house who would give me work selling newspapers. I went there but she didn't want to take me on. So I asked Felipe: 'Where can I go?' and he said: 'The Sotano – that's where the orphans are, and you'll have a better time.' "

For Jose-Roberto the Sotano has meant starting a new life.

"Here in the Sotano it's like being in your own home," he says. "You clean, help to wash the dishes, cook...and the Sales-

SOTANO: 'They welcomed me like a brother. I was very happy.'

ians...they're very good with us. They're like our parents – our second parents. They send kids to San Patricio after three months if they behave themselves. I guess I behaved myself really well because they sent me after a month and a half. They said if I stayed there in the Sotano I'd get messed up.

"In the Sotano the kids said we would be beaten here at San Patricio if we were stupid. They told us stories to make us not want to come. I came here with that fear – will they hit me or won't they? Will I fight or won't I? But no, they don't hit anyone. All of that was just a story. They welcomed me like a brother, like one more brother in the San Patricio family. That was what I liked the best. In the chapel they welcomed us with some songs. That was the happiest moment of my life."

At San Patricio Jose-Roberto started learning carpentry and mechanics, then became an apprentice electrician.

"I'm in the first course, which is about domestic installations. Then I'll go on to the second course, which is a bit more advanced. We'll learn about the paging systems that you find in some places, that let you talk within the building from upstairs. Then there'll be industrial installations in the third course. By the time I complete the sixth course, I'll even be able to wire turbines. If I can, I want to finish here before I'm called up for military service at 18."

Jose-Roberto is very aware of how much he has matured since he first arrived at the Sotano.

"I've changed a lot. I'm more grown up now. Before I was quite quiet. Now I'm less so. Before I went without money. I was quite a mess. Now I can go out with the allowance that they give us and I can buy myself things. And I can go out in good clothes because here they give us clothes, though we have to work for them.

"But what I would still really like to do is go back to secondary school and get my High School Diploma. Then I could go to university to study to be a veterinary surgeon. I like little animals. People sometimes try to kill them, but that's not for me. I like to care for them."

Sadly among the shoe-shine boys of Quito, Jose-Roberto is an exception. Few share his aspirations or his prospects. More, many more, are like Edison.

TAMMY: THE NEWSPAPERGIRL

'When me mum and dad told me they'd put my name down for a round, I weren't right amused. I were a bit horrified'

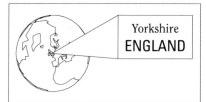

Yorkshire
ENGLAND

'MY NAME is Tammy. When I first started at secondary school I only got one pound pocket money. It wasn't enough really as I'd started a new hobby going, keeping fish. One time, after I'd been moaning at them, me mum and dad went up to town and saw an advert in the shop window of the newsagents asking for a paper boy or girl. It were a Sunday round. When they told me they'd put my name down for it I weren't right amused. In fact, I were a bit horrified.

At first my Dad used to help me, taking the papers round in the car. But that got a bit much so my brother Mark started to help me. He'd carry half the bag while I carried the other half. I did the Sunday round for a while and then a weekday round came up, so now I'm doing both. When I get up I get dressed and if my mum's down I have a cup of tea. Then I get my bag and I set off. Outside the solicitor's there's always a lot of worms on the path. I can't stand worms, so I have to dodge the worms before I can get to the letter-box. It's a right big letter-box and it snaps. Then I have to dodge all the worms going back out again. A couple of days ago I got my fingers trapped in that letter-box and it were painful. Then up on the estate there's a house with a new dog – they've only had it a couple of weeks. It's a right queer one because it comes up to the door when you're putting the paper in and head-butts the door. Then it takes the paper out of the letter-box and starts chewing it up. So all you see is paper flying about. Then there's the old man at No 61. He wears Hawaiian shirts and straw hats. He's a right chubby old fella who comes out in a morning, or if it's cold he just stays in his window and waves to me. He gave me a Christmas bonus.

Then there's this lad, works for a different shop and crosses through my round. I don't fancy the look of him. He reckons he's well hard. Once our Mark nearly had a fight with him. Ever since I've walked straight past him, I don't say hello or nowt and we just walk past each other. But I always have a paper ready to hit him if he starts. After the round's finished I come back home in time to watch *Caspar The Ghost* on telly. I get my breakfast if I fancy owt. If not I don't bother. Then I go into the kitchen, wash-up, leave Mark to dry up. At about eight o'clock I set off to meet Marnie, Emma and Kelly at the Esso garage and we walk on to school.

I get £5.50 for doing about 20 papers on the weekly round, that's with a bonus if I do all the papers right and get in on time for the full week. And then when I go on my Sunday round I get about 70 papers to deliver. For them I earn about £4, so overall for the week I get £9.50. I'm supposed to put £4 in the bank, which is to save for my holiday in Corfu. The rest I spend on felt pictures for my bedroom, and I've been saving up for my fish. I've got three fish but they've outgrown their tank, which is not fair on them. I went to the shop to get another tank but they were right expensive. So I asked the man if he had any others and he went upstairs and found one that was an unusual size. He said it was £15 but I could have it for £10.'

DOING THE ROUNDS: 'I save £4 a week for my holiday and spend the rest on my fish.'

YASSER: APPRENTICE BAKER

'My brother suggested I work with them on the counter, but I said I wanted to learn the trade at the back of the shop'

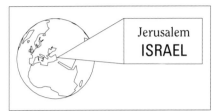

Jerusalem
ISRAEL

YASSER lives in an established Arab community on the fringe of East Jerusalem. He is part of a very large family, headed by his very elderly father. At twelve, Yasser is the youngest child with five older brothers and three sisters. All the brothers work in the bakery set up by the father when he was young. Several now have their own children and one of these, three-year-old Karim, regularly helps by stacking bread. Most of the family live together in an apartment block built by the father. Under Israeli law, Yasser should still be at school. But he found learning to read and write difficult and he knew there was the opportunity to join the family business, become a master baker, and gradually take over responsibility for its management. Yasser is not working out of economic necessity. His family is moderately prosperous, he gets paid generous pocket-money, and his work is not too hard.

MY NAME is Yasser al-Khateeb. I have always helped my brothers in the bakery, stacking bread, just like little Karim does now.

I was at school until I was ten years old. School was better than work, but I left because I wasn't very clever.

The day after I left school, my brother suggested I work with them on the counter. But I said I wanted to learn the trade at the back of the shop. He agreed to teach me but he said I should continue as cashier so I agreed.

I don't take a wage from my brothers. They give me pocket-money on Fridays – 40 shekels for the week *{about £13}*.

I don't read a lot. If someone brings a newspaper when I'm on the counter, I'll read the important bits, the headlines, that's all. Then I get bored and put the paper away. I am much better at reckoning than I am at reading. I'm at my best in arithmetic.

For instance, someone came to the counter and gave me a hundred shekels. He asked for ten pitot breads and asked me how much change was due to him. I totted it up and told him 98 – no, 97 shekels and 800 agarot.

Besides Arabic, I know a little Hebrew and a bit of English. If someone says: 'Good morning' I'll say: 'Good morning' back. If someone asks me: 'How much is this pitot?' I'll say: 'Two hundred and fifty'. I also know a bit of French, just one or two words.

First of all at seven o'clock in the morning I come down with my brother Hussein. We bring flour to put in the machine. Then we pour in a bag of sugar. Then a bag of yeast and then some salt – all this to get the dough to rise and get bigger. Then we add the water and start the machine. Next I bring in firewood and put it in the oven to dry out for ten minutes. Then I put some pieces of paper under the wood and light them. I wait until the wood is glowing and giving off heat without flames. Then I shut the oven and leave it. When all the dough has been thoroughly mixed we stop the machine and wait. My brother Faisal goes upstairs to make tea. We sit and have a cup of tea while the dough is rising. Then we bring the dough out, Hussein and me, and start kneading it into lengths.

We put it on to the bench and chop it up into portions until we have filled four or five trays with loaves. Faisal rolls them out into pitot shapes while Hussein cuts the dough and I fold it. Next we put the pitot breads on to the oven paddles and leave them to settle for fifteen minutes. Then we bake them. When they are ready I go to get Karim to help stack the breads. I take a trayful upstairs to sell in the shop. Once they're sold I come back down for more and so on. Once the first batch of dough is finished we start on the second batch. For this one we put in two or two-and-a-half bags of flour, two or two-and-a-half

WORKER: 'I don't read a lot. I'm better at sums.'

packets of yeast, one to one-and-a-half packets of sugar, perhaps two packets of salt, and two or two-and-a-half pinches of baking powder.

When the second dough has been mixed we have a break, just like before, then we knead it. This is when my other brothers come. Youssef and Abdullah. Abdullah is the one who pulls the dough out into lengths. Faisal cuts it up and puts it on the bench. Then we let Abdullah fold the dough and roll it out. He fills up six trays, then Youssef and Hussein pat them out flat and put them on the paddles ready for the oven. Then comes the third batch. We have to start the third batch half-way through the second batch, before it has been put on the paddles to rise. We make a mixture as before, add water and start the machine. Once the third batch is mixed we leave it and go back to baking the second batch. When the bread is ready I do just the same as before.

Karim stacks the breads and I take them up to sell. I make many trips up and down the stairs carrying the trays of bread to the shop. Once the second batch is finished we start working again on the third batch. We roll them into loaves or into extra large pitots. They are left for a very long time so the dough can settle and the yeast can breathe...for an hour or two. Then they are baked and after that half are taken to the restaurant and the other half are left for me to sell at the counter.

I stay until all the bread is sold. Then I close up the bakery, clean and tidy the place up. I bring in all the wooden paddles and trays. I lock up and take the key with me. Then I go home at about six-thirty with my brothers. We get washed, put on our pyjamas, and go to bed.

JARRY: THE CANE-CUTTER

'We only have one meal a day. My mother usually cooks some rice. When I get hungry during the day, I cut open one of the canes and suck on it'

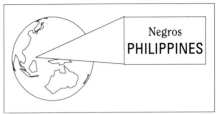

Negros
PHILIPPINES

'MY NAME is Jarry. I live and work with my mother and father on a big sugar plantation on the island of Negros in the Philippines. I have six brothers and four sisters. My parents cannot earn enough to support all of us. So I had to leave school.

I went to school long enough to learn to read and write, but I still find it very difficult to write. Even when I was at school I always worked on the plantation when I had free time and during holidays.

Now I work all day, six days a week. I usually get up at five o'clock in the morning and get a little breakfast. Then I go on to the plantation at seven o'clock and work through until five o'clock in the afternoon.

My job right now is to follow on the cane-cutters, trimming the canes, stacking them and then loading them on the trucks. Other times I do planting and weeding. We don't own any land ourselves. We only earn money when they give us work to do. I can earn fifteen pesos a day *{about 45p}*. But sometimes I earn nothing.

We only have one meal a day. In the evening my mother usually cooks some rice. When I get hungry during the day I just cut open one of the canes and suck on it.

I expect one day I will become a cane-cutter like my father. There isn't much else I can do.

FUTURE: 'I expect one day I'll be a cane-cutter. There's not much else I can do.'

CHAPTER FIVE: SCHOOL

SIMEON: THE FIRST DAY

A game of football, a picture of Humpty Dumpty, a rubber that won't work and a bit of help from the oldest boy in school

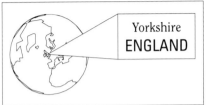

Yorkshire
ENGLAND

IT WAS a big day for four-year-old Simeon – his first afternoon at school. He was about to start at one of the smallest schools in England, a picture-book building of local stone under a steeply pitched, slate roof. There is only one classroom with just seventeen children, so newcomers sit side by side with eleven-year-olds who are nearly ready for secondary school. Most of the children live in or near the village, but a few are brought in each day from outlying farms. There is quite a family atmosphere. Many of the children have played together on The Green since infancy and several learn alongside brothers, sisters and cousins. Simeon is no exception. Six-year-old Amy is already well established in the school. Their father Jonty, too, remembers what he used to get up to around the schoolyard many years ago.

So starting school for Simeon was far less daunting than for many of the half million British children who go through the ritual each year. He was already well used to making the short journey from home to school. He has walked it twice a day for as long as he can remember, delivering or collecting Amy. But this time was different. This time he was staying.

"I can see Jacob, Emma and Sandra," he called out as they came around the corner. On their first day, children attend only for the afternoon and start by joining in lunchtime play. By the time they reached the gates, it had already begun to bustle. Now was the moment for Simeon's mum to hand him over to his teacher. Fiona was not at all sure how her strong-willed but sensitive little boy would react to being left for the first time. She was eager not to prolong the goodbyes for fear that Simeon might change his mind about the whole idea. Bending down she delivered him a quick kiss and then hurried away with little brother Edward. She needn't have worried. There was no way that Simeon's young pride would have let him make a scene in front of his sister and all the other children.

Left on his own, Simeon seemed bewildered by the boisterous activity that surrounded him and unsure what to do next. He slowly swung round and sized up the playground. Seventeen children on a small area of tarmac bear no comparison to the heavily-populated spaces of city schools. But to a four-year-old it is still quite a crowd.

Simeon made for the security of a wall to climb up and sit on. He was not left alone for long, as several girls peeled off from their circle game of The Farmer's In The Dell.

A girl with pigtails was first to inspect the newcomer. Grabbing hold of Simeon's short legs dangling off the wall, she waggled them about.

"Get off," protested Simeon, trying to appear disinterested.

The girl tried another line. "How old are you, Simeon?"

"Four."

His reply was echoed back immediately: "Four – 1, 2, 3, 4." Not satisfied, the girl made another attempt to provoke the new boy. "How old are you again?"

But this time she did not wait for an answer, grabbing his feet and pumping them vigorously up and down in time with her chanting: "1, 2, 3, 4, 5, 6, 7, 8, 9, 10, 11, 12, 13, 14, 15, 16, 17, 18, 19, 100."

By now the spectacle had attracted quite a crowd. One of the smallest stepped forward and offered Simeon some support.

"I'm four, too," he said.

Simeon was not sure quite how to handle all this attention. He responded with all the toughness he could manage. "Will everybody get out of the way and don't crowd me!"

Fortunately for Simeon the oldest boy in the school, James, had noticed what was going on. An improbably uneven pattern of local birth in

NEW BOY: Simeon finds his place.

recent years meant that there were only four boys on the school roll. Under these circumstances a male reinforcement was a welcome addition, even if he was only four.

"Would you like to play football," he asked Simeon.

No hesitation. "I would," came the reply.

Simeon liked the idea of joining a game that he had only ever been able to watch through the railings in the past. Then, suddenly, playtime was over. The children were summoned into the classroom. But Simeon did not forget his older friend. James helped Simeon hang up his coat and then he was led over to his desk. Simeon sat wondering what to do next, then asked his neighbour, who turned out to be Bryce, the other four-year-old he had met in the playground. He did not have to wait long before the assistant teacher came over to get him started. He was quickly presented with his first exercise book and pencil and packet of crayons.

"Do you know any nursery rhymes?" asked his teacher. Simeon hesitated, then defensively said he did not, but with a little encouragement admitted knowing Jack And Jill and Humpty Dumpty and was set to work drawing a picture.

Simeon worked quietly for some time, feet dangling down from his oversized chair. Then his teacher came to him for a second time and said: "Simeon, would you like to go with James and he'll show you where to put your towel."

"I haven't got a towel!" he exclaimed without noticing the blue towel that his teacher was carrying. The other children laughed, but again James came to the rescue. He took Simeon by the hand and led him out of the building to the toilets out in the schoolyard. Some days later, Fiona was to get a surprise when Simeon arrived back at the cottage in the middle of the morning and hurried to the upstairs bathroom. The door to the school toilets had defeated him and, unknown to his teacher, he had headed for the only other one he knew about.

Back in the classroom a few minutes later on that first day, Simeon carried on with his drawing of Humpty Dumpty. Simeon had spent much of the summer out on the fells with his

OUTSIDE IN: The other side of the railings.

father, helping him to repair dry stone walls. He always felt more at home with a pick-axe in his hand than a crayon. So when he made a mistake on the very first picture in his new school exercise book, he was not at all sure what to do about it. He appealed to the girl with pigtails at the desk behind, who offered a rubber. But that only seemed to make things worse.

"I can't rub out with it," he whispered back to the girl as the paper became more and more rumpled and the colours smudged. She tried to show Simeon how to hold the paper firmly while using only one corner of the rubber. He tried again and, satisfied that he had done the best he could, threw the rubber down on to the desk in disgust.

It was almost time for afternoon break. James kept his promise to let Simeon join in the game of football. "Give it a slogger," Simeon was advised but, when the ball came his way, he missed it altogether. Undaunted he tried again, shouting to James to pass him the ball. And when someone accidentally kicked it right into his face, he shouted: "You hit me on the head and I'll punch you one."

The rest of that first afternoon was uneventful – a game with Lego followed by a story. Then Fiona pushed the pram back to the school gate at three o'clock. Simeon was already waiting in the school lobby and seemed relieved to see his mother. But he was not going to budge until he had been dismissed by his teacher. There is a clear demarcation line between the authority of home and school. That much Simeon had already learned on Day One.

"Have you had a nice time?" asked Fiona. Simeon seemed especially eager to be close to his mother and helped her push the pram. "What have you been doing?" she asked him.

"I did a beautiful picture of Humpty Dumpty and our garden, but I can't bring it home."

Beyond that, Simeon did not seem to want to talk about his first day at school. Fiona, relieved that it seemed to have gone quite well, left it at that.

"After all," she said, "he's got many more schooldays to come."

DRAW: *Here's how it's done.*

OOPS: *I can't get this rubber to work.*

LIKE THIS: *'I did a beautiful picture of Humpty Dumpty, but I can't bring it home.'*

MAXIMINO: MAKING SCHOOL WORK

'Before I go to school I have to feed the rabbits and hens, tether the baby goats, feed the calf, fetch firewood and split it and sometimes do jobs for my father'

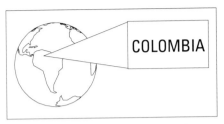

COLOMBIA

AT MAXIMINO'S school the children are in charge. They vote for the organising committees and the School President, who is currently a delicate-looking little girl called Daisy.

At Maximino's school hours of attendance are not fixed. They are flexible, negotiated with individual children according to their family circumstances and other commitments.

And at Maximino's school it is the pupils who organise most of the teaching, working in cooperative groups on a curriculum that is closely linked to the interests of their community.

If Maximino were not at this kind of school, he would probably not go to school at all. Even though he is only eleven he would probably have already failed or dropped out.

And where might such a radical school as Maximino's be found? Serving an alternative community in the South West of England, perhaps? Or satisfying the idealistic theories of a group of ageing Californian hippies? Maximino's school certainly sounds like the latest esoteric clone of A. S. Neill's Summerhill, but it could not be further away either culturally or economically.

Maximino's school is perched on the top of a mountain in one of the poorest countries on earth, Colombia in Latin America. It is one of 8,000 Escuelas Nuevas, or New Schools, dotted around in tiny rural communities throughout the country. Colombia is well known for its murderous drug barons and unstable governments. It seems an unlikely setting for one of the most promising innovations in progressive education to emerge this decade. Yet this Latin American initiative has become a model for countries as far apart as Senegal and Honduras, China and Paraguay.

There is nothing unusual about Maximino. He is a very bright and well-adjusted youngster. He is also a typical Escuela Nueva child. He comes from a farming family and lives in a ramshackle farmhouse built out of local sun-baked bricks with a corrugated iron roof. The village is at the centre of a small fertile plateau, precariously set among dramatic mountain peaks and only accessible by a steep, narrow track. Like virtually all the villagers, Maximino's family survive mainly by growing subsistence crops of maize, beans, potatoes and a few coffee bushes. They have only one major cash crop – hybrid blackberries.

Looking out from the windows of the simple school building, the landscape is festooned with wires supporting the tangle of vines. Cultivating blackberries is a slow, labour-intensive and prickly business and Maximino's parents depend on each of their children to help out with the crops. Their work is especially important at harvest time when itinerant dealers haul their trucks up the mountainside to buy fruits at low prices and sell them for fat profits in the markets of the capital Bogota. With all this work to be done, Maximino cannot just crawl out of bed, grab a bowl of cornflakes and wander off to school.

"In the morning, before I go to school I have to do many jobs to help my family. I have to cut

IN CLASS: 'We work together, so when someone doesn't understand they ask a friend.'

grass to feed the rabbits and the hens and give them water. Next, I take the baby goats out and tether them. Then I have the calf to feed. Sometimes I fetch firewood and split it, or my father may call me somewhere else to do a different job. All of this can take me until it's time to go to school. Then when I get out of school at lunchtime I come back, have lunch, take off my school clothes and go and work with my father wherever he is, whatever he wants me to do. But if he sends for me at school to come and help, I come home even sooner.

"Sometimes I have to go on the bus on some urgent errand, or at harvest time I have to be at home to help pick the blackberries if there is no one else around to do it. Then I have to miss school altogether, because I have to help them out."

Conventional schools organised on European lines would find it difficult to accept the demands made by Maximino's father on his son's school time. He would soon become another missing face, falling behind the other children. In many parts of the world he would be forced to repeat a whole school year, then another and another, until he might become a demoralised 12-year-old expected to sit in a classroom alongside children barely half his age. The Escuela Nueva, by contrast, does not impose full-time attendance on the children, but recognises that school must be integrated into the other pressures on a rural child's time.

"When I miss lessons, I can ask to borrow The Guide and catch up that way. Then I don't have to ask about all that they have done while I've been off school. Of course, if I missed three or four months, then I'd get very behind."

The Guide is one of many practical features of this school. Textbooks, pencils, rulers, exercise books and especially teachers are all something of a luxury. So in the Escuela Nueva pupils are encouraged to take responsibility for organising their work from an early age with the help of a few copies of a national curriculum guide that they share. One of the originators of the Escuela Nueva, Vicky Colbert, describes this as "a sort of Open University approach to Primary Education." It certainly appeals to Maximino.

"In the classrooms we learn in groups. In the fourth year there are two groups, one working with one copy of The Guidebook and the other with a second copy. We work together on our lessons. So when somebody doesn't understand something they ask a friend in their group. So if

HOMEWORK: *Maximino and his father plant a tree to stop soil erosion.*

I know the answer I explain it to them and they do the same when they know the answer and are asked. But if none of us understands, we can ask the teacher. I like this method. It's very good because you learn a lot."

The Escuela Nueva draws its values from the community itself. It is designed to reflect the issues and problems that face a rural farming community and help the children to tackle them when they grow older. Take soil erosion, for example. It is a massive problem in Maximino's village as in many other parts of the world, so it is a major topic in his schooling, and not just in theory. Having learned the basic principles, Maximino's homework is to put them into practice. This is no problem. His family's farmland includes a steep-sided gorge where the topsoil is literally peeling away from the rock beneath and sliding down into the stream. Maximino has spent many afternoons working with his father to plant eucalyptus trees at the top of the gorge.

Another, and perhaps the most remarkable, feature of the Escuela Nueva is the extent to which children are encouraged to take shared responsibility for most aspects of school life. As Maximino explains: "In the Escuela Nueva we have a school government to help us learn to cooperate. So any boy who is playing about or making a nuisance is sent to the appropriate committee to be sorted out accordingly.

"There are various committees, such as the vegetable-gardening committee, the flower-gardening committee, the library committee, the Red Cross committee and the cleaning-up

NEW SCHOOL: 'We elect the school government, president and committees.'

committee. I work on the cleaning-up committee and we have to keep the school clean. We have to move the desks about, sweep up, clean and dust the classrooms and corridors, as well as the toilets. Then we have to pick up all the litter and take it well away from the school to burn it."

The focal point of government at the Escuela Nueva is the morning assembly. The children are in charge with the teachers watching from the back. School uniform is one of the few conventions in such a radical system of education, with boys wearing smart shirts and shorts and girls in tartan dresses. As usual the assembly is presided over by the young President Daisy, who invites each committee leader to report in turn. It is an unlikely part of the world to find such a high level of commitment to democracy.

"We elect the school government by secret ballot. There's a president and vice-president to organise the committees and leaders at each level. The one with the most votes is the President, the next is the vice-President. The leaders of each committee are chosen in the same way. Then there are the monitors. They are chosen by the children in each year group."

President Daisy seems too small to command the respect of such a large group of children, many of whom are head and shoulders taller than she is. But she makes up for lack of height with a loud voice. She leads the assembly in reciting the school anthem: 'I am a student. My life is here working in the New School. Long live my school. Long live the New School. There are many schools but few like this one; under our control and with its own library. We always decide what we think and feel. We've started it all ourselves and the parents have helped.'

Maximino thrives in a school he can understand and feel comfortable in. So comfortable, that he can even start planning for the future with more than a little ambition. "When I'm grown up," he says, "I'd like to set up a business, a factory or something, or perhaps buy a property in Bogota or here in the country."

LUKE: THE ENTRANCE EXAM

'They have to, like, find out who can take it in. I mean if they're teaching people that just don't understand it, then they're wasting their time really'

Manchester
ENGLAND

LUKE is hoping to go to Manchester Grammar School, but first he has to attend an entrance examination.

'Well I was impressed. I was very impressed. It looks a very good school. Also, it looks like a very big school. They said there's roughly fifteen hundred boys in the school, and that's a fairly big number when you've been in a school of about seven hundred. It's almost – it's over double what I'm used to. My mum brought me in the car. When we got to the gate the prefect reminded my mum that she couldn't go beyond this point. So she said goodbye and good luck and I set off up the drive.

I found a seat in the hall and then we were divided into different schools and split up into three classes. I was in D. We were put in little groups of about five and guided by the prefects into the classrooms. We were given seats in alphabetical order. It started at one side and continued for about four lines. Because my surname's Stubbs, I was sitting in the very end row.

I was expecting the classroom walls to be covered with posters of Einstein's theory of relativity and physics charts and stuff like that, but there was pictures of Hell's Angels going through the Arizona Desert on dragsters. That gave me a fairly funny impression and there was also news sheets about trekking, and I think there was a map of the world.

It was fifty minutes for the first paper and there was seventy questions. He suggested we flicked through to see that we didn't miss any pages. Most of the boys finished with about five or ten minutes to spare. I finished with about ten minutes to spare, so I went back and checked over and corrected a few answers that I thought were wrong just in the last minute.

I told my mum and dad how many I answered and whether I think I've got a chance or not. I'm fairly confident. As we went out, the teacher told us that the results would be given in the middle of the week following the exam. I'm just hoping at the moment.'

Luke passed the first stage of the selection process.

'If you're requested to sit the second stage then you've got a chance of getting through. I think it's a good idea, because if you've not gone through then you've got other schools to turn to, or your 11-Plus results.

I reckon that the second part is going to be quite a bit more difficult. I've become familiar with the place, but we might be changing to different surroundings and also it's a completely different paper with harder questions. I've had some trial ones and I've been practising. They're different – more complex. One of them I had to do was a poem about a mother and son peeling the potatoes and about the peels falling into a bucket of water. It said: 'Describe the falling of the peel into the bucket of water – the sound and feeling of it.' And there were others about a willow tree hanging over a stream and also pebbles falling into a river or bucket.

My teacher has given me some more practice papers to do over the next week, especially maths. I'm absolutely hopeless at long division and decimals and dividing and multiplying fractions. I can add them and subtract them but I'm no hope at the other two. But I've been gradually picking up over the last three years or so, and I think I've got the hang of them. But I need more practice before the day comes.

CHANGE: 'I've never been to an all-boys school.'

I think that there's a certain higher standard of education there at Manchester Grammar. They have to, like, find out who can get through it. I mean if they're teaching people that just don't take it in, and when they're older just don't understand it, then they're wasting their time really. It's just determining what children have the ability and what children don't, I think.

It will be different certainly because I've never been in surroundings where it's all boys. Also it will take me a while to become familiar with the place because, well, the looks of it. It looks quite big after primary school. There isn't the same nice atmosphere, being all mixed and things. I mean, it's better to have girls and boys. Like William Hulme Grammar School has just merged, but I don't know whether Manchester Grammar will because it's got a reputation for boys. I don't know if it'll start giving girls education. But we'll be gaining as well as losing, because we'll be going on hikes and treks and things like that. But I've been at Flixton Primary School for a while and I know that I'll miss the place. I'll miss it – the atmosphere and things.

Luke passed the second stage and was accepted into the school.

TAATSKE: AT A STEINER SCHOOL

'Daddy says girls once were only given knitting to do and boys manual work, so it's nice that we get both. Most of the time I play with the boys.'

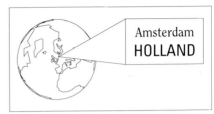

Amsterdam
HOLLAND

ONE look at the blackboard in Taatske's classroom is enough to tell you that this is no ordinary school. This blackboard is a work of art. There are no lines of writing or sums drawn in endless rows of white chalk. Instead, there is a brightly-coloured picture of the four points of the compass in one area and a large desert landscape in another, with words of explanation neatly presented all around.

Taatske's teacher, Joly, has been working with them on a Main Lesson in geography, one example of the educational method devised by an Austrian scientist, philosopher and visionary called Rudolf Steiner. More than 80 years ago, Steiner set out to change the face of schools. He said: "Our highest endeavour must be to develop free human beings who are able to impart purpose and direction to their lives."

TAATSKE: Lively mind in a lively school.

Steiner once described modern civilisation as like a head full of pigeon-holed ideas, dangling in space without any clear connection to bodily feelings or actions. He worked untiringly to promote a more balanced vision of developing humanity, which would integrate art with science, intellect with feeling, academic with practical, and the spiritual with the physical. Steiner's vision has become influential in fields as diverse as agriculture, medicine and business as well as education.

His first school was set up in Stuttgart in 1919 for workers' children at the Waldorf-Astoria cigarette factory. Steiner wanted to help children to develop their skills and qualities more fully. In recent years the movement has been growing fast. Taatske's school is in Amsterdam and there are now more then three hundred Waldorf schools in countries as far apart as Argentina and Australia, Finland and France, not forgetting England, Ireland, Scotland and Wales. Waldorf schools are especially well established in Holland and Germany, supported with substantial government funding.

The core of the curriculum is the daily Main Lesson. Taatske and her friends work on the same

CLASS: 'Joly is both a teacher and a friend, not just Miss in front of the class.'

topic, theme or project for two hours each morning and for several weeks at a time. Waldorf schools have no time for the commonly-held belief that young children have a short attention span and need to change topic frequently. Nor do they place too much emphasis on teaching purely through 'talk and chalk' as Taatske's teacher explains: "I try to develop the whole personality of each child. The content of what I am teaching is not an aim in itself, but a way to help them to develop themselves. Even in Class 5 we do a lot of practical things to try to help their learning. I've been introducing decimals, which I try to do together with movements. Like I throw a ball and say: 'One tenth' and the person who catches the ball must say: '0.1'. It helps to memorize that there is a connection between body and mind, and also it's nice to do. It's fun."

Taatske is still alongside the same children she started kindergarten with at the age of four, and she will stay with them until she leaves school at 18. Boys and girls are encouraged to learn side by side in a wide range of academic and practical subjects. They have no prejudice about which are "boys' subjects" and which "girls' subjects". They all do knitting and wood carving and metalwork and gardening and games.

Taatske says: "I once heard Daddy say that it used not to be like that. In those days the girls were only given knitting to do and the boys were given manual work, so I find it quite nice that we are given both of these things to do. Most of the time I play with the boys because most go and play football or something like that. Sometimes I play with the girls or simply with everybody when we're playing a game like Kick The Can."

At the centre of this approach to education is the pupils' relationship to their teacher. Joly is not Taatske's teacher just for the year. They will be together for most of her school life.

"I've been Taatske's teacher ever since she was six, and the class will stay with me for eight years until they are fourteen," says Joly. "It's a big responsibility I feel towards them, to teach them everything and to give them love. One big advantage is that you come to know each other so well. I go to their homes, I know their parents, I understand their situation a bit. I think the parents trust me and the children – they love me and they'll work for me. They feel safe when they are together with one person for such a long time. And that's important in today's society. It means one day they can hate me very much, but the next day it can be good again. All these emotions are allowed and it's still safe."

TREE HOUSE: 'Dad and I built the platform.'

Taatske says: "I think Joly is both a teacher and a friend. It's not as though you think all the time that this is 'Miss' who stands in front of the class and that's the end of it. I mean you can also talk to her about other things, it doesn't have to be always about sums. You can talk to her about something funny that happened at home for example."

The result of all this is that Taatske is a bright, lively girl, always full of questions and ideas, always making something out of nothing and never bothered about getting her hands dirty. She goes to school on a battered old bike, rattling down backstreets, jumping off to cross over busy tramways, and taking shortcuts across canal footbridges. Taatske painted the bike herself and she is proud of it. She oils the chain and mends the punctures with just a little help from her Dad. It is only her going-to-school bike. She keeps her racer safe at home in the family's ground-floor apartment, or even in her bedroom when she is allowed, alongside her woodworking tools, her collection of electronic bits and her gerbil.

Earlier in the summer Taatske wanted to build a tree house in her tiny overgrown garden. "I was given the tree house for my birthday. Well, actually, I only got the wood for my birthday – the tent came later. My Dad and I made it together, and that was fun. We fixed three wooden posts against the tree and then built a platform on top. Then we fixed a rope ladder to climb into the tent. Most of the time I go up there to read. I always take a pillow up there with me, filled with the things I need. Climbing up can be quite difficult, because I'm afraid of dropping something. But once I get inside I like it. I mean, I'm on my own and I find that quite cosy. I like zipping everything up. Doing up the tent-zip makes me feel I'm on holiday. Zipping-up my sleeping bag makes a holiday-like sound too. I like to climb into it with a pillow for my head and start reading. Sometimes I try to do my homework in the tent. I can do arithmetic or something like that, but not writing – that isn't so easy."

Taatske was quite late learning to read and write, but not from any lack of ability. In a world that is obsessed with introducing children to the 3 Rs at the earliest opportunity, Waldorf schools prefer to wait until they are at least six years old. The argument is that, while it is perfectly possible to teach these skills at an early age, to do so hurries children into forms of abstract, adult thinking at a time when their energies are more naturally spent mastering the challenges of their more immediate surroundings. Widespread literacy is, after all, only a very recent feature of human civilisation. Why impose it on children who have barely left behind their infancy? This appeals to Taatske's mother.

HIGH NOTE: 'Music's enjoyable, except practice.'

"If they are slow in reading and arithmetic at school, never mind. They'll learn it anyway. Most children have to learn reading at four or five years old. I think it's a pity. It draws their energy too early into an abstract way of thinking. They can read all their lives, whereas the intuitive phase of life is only rather short."

It was for similar reasons that Taatske's family discouraged much TV viewing while she was young. They felt it would expose her to all kinds of inappropriate and incomprehensible images and encourage her to be passive.

Taatske has just started on a new hobby, too. "I've started to play the tuba," she says. "I hit on that idea because a friend of mine played it as well. Every evening I go to the Young Excelsior Society, which is an orchestra. I find music quite enjoyable, except sometimes when I have to go and practise. Best of all I like playing a duet with my friend. I do that every day and it's nice, especially when a circle of people forms round us and they applaud. Then I think: 'Ugh! I'll have to practise again before going to play the orchestra'."

BELINDA: SCHOOL OF THE AIR

'The teacher is 100 miles away. We send in our books on a Friday and they mark them and send them back on mail day'

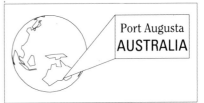

MY NAME is Belinda Anne Rowe. I'm ten years old and I come from Mount Elm Sheep Station, which is in the Flinders Ranges in South Australia. I've got two sisters. Danielle's five and Lisa's seven. Like me they're both in the School of the Air.

The School of the Air is actually a school for isolated children that live out in the Bush – that are in a place where they can't really get to a regular school. So we have 'air' lessons over the radio. The teacher is at Port Augusta, about 100 miles away. The teacher talks to the children and they talk back even though the teachers don't get to see them. Every so often they might come out and see them on a visit or when they go meet at a children's camp.

In the morning we go to our little school room at 8.45. It's in the old sheep shearers' quarters and is really just a wooden shed. When we get there we turn the radio on and listen to what we should do. There's assembly on Monday which tells us all the messages and who's got work on the display board. There's also problem-solving and station profile. Station profile means you write in and tell the class what the Bush station you're living on is like. Then at nine o'clock we do silent reading and at half past nine we do language. Then we do various things until eleven and then maths until half past eleven, and then spelling until twelve.

You send in your maths book and your language book and your spelling books and all those kind of books that children in normal schools have. We send them in on a Friday night and they mark them on Mondays and Tuesdays and then they send them back again on mail day. We also have a governess who lives with us. She's called Miss Sandy and is a really good governess. She's not actually a qualified teacher, she just doles out the work they've set. But if you've got a problem she helps you, like if an air lesson's on. Normally it's only Danielle and Lisa she helps. I can handle my lesson myself.

After primary school I'll be going away to boarding school in Port Augusta. You can stay on with School of the Air – like there was one kid, he stayed on till grade 11 and 12. But most children go away to boarding school after Grade 7.

In the afternoons we normally help Dad. Like yesterday we were mustering sheep for crutching – that's trimming the wool round their rears to stop them getting diseases. You have to go out into the paddocks and bring them in. Then we help Mum sweep and make beds and deal with the chickens and feed the cattle and do lots of other chores, like chopping wood, especially in winter time. There's a lot of other jobs, like we sometimes help Dad do lamb-tailing and we might even help him do a fence or something like that.

Dad's taught us to drive the Daihatsu so that if maybe a sheep gets away or something and dad's out chasing him on the motorbike and it gets away, we can drive out to get it. Or say dad's doing the troughs and he may not really feel like driving. We can drive for him. It's a good thing we've learned earlier than most children do.

PEACE: Belinda finds time to do a little reading in the calm of the sheep station.

MOTORING: 'If a sheep gets away, we can drive out to get it for Dad.'

PLAY AND DISCOVERY

Let's pretend

THE best toy in the world is a good imagination. It turns a cardboard box into a spaceship, cupboards into castles and back gardens into enchanted forests. Amy and little Jenny imagine they are witches weaving spells and charms. "We're making a potion to stop Daddy snoring," says Amy. "Jenny helped by fetching me things. She got some soil, some chippings, a little man, some water and a spoon."

Imagination and fantasy can be bought, too. These interactive video guns 'shoot' at the screen, but the screen can 'shoot' back and make the boys' guns fall apart in their hands. Once the electronic barrier is overcome, the imagination can take over once again.

Do it yourself

YOU don't need much for a game. All you need to play Nsolo (above) is a stick to draw a Union Jack grid in the sand, and six pebbles, twigs or leaves to act as counters. The loser in this Zambian 'board game' is the first player who cannot move one of his pieces to an empty space.

In Sao Paulo, Brazil a few pieces of wood nailed together, a couple of wheels and you have a cart just like grown-ups use. Copying adults is an important part of playing. Children can learn in a safe and enjoyable way and try out the skills that they will need when they are older.

The skateboarders

ON THE BOARD: Elbow pads, knee pads, helmet – all you need to travel in real comfort.

IN THE STICKS: The same toy stripped down to the bones, and the owner is just as proud.

Skip and clap and jump, as

Eeny-meeny-mack-aracka,
Air-eye-domin-acker,
Chicka-bocka-om-pom-push!

THE girls in a playground in Melbourne, Australia may think that their rhyme is just a piece of nonsense. But it is recognisable throughout the English-speaking world. The song is never written down by the children, nor taught by parents or teachers, but it spreads and lasts and thrives. There are many more, sung and chanted to skipping and clapping games or, like the one above, for choosing someone to be 'it'.

Elastics is a variation on skipping, using rings of elastic to jump in and out of instead of a rope to turn. A favourite elastics rhyme is: 'England, Ireland, Scotland, Wales. Inside, outside, puppy dogs' tails.'

the marbles craze rolls on

Blood Royals, Rainbow Pearls, Ghost Lasers and Tom Birdcages – they all have a different value to the dedicated marbles fan in the playground or park...

MARBLES has its own season that usually starts roughly half-way through February and goes on for about two months. As crazes come and crazes go, the art of collecting and playing marbles rolls on year after year after year. In Australia, the smallest are called *pee-wees*, then come *ordinaries*, *half-semis* and *semis*. The biggest are the *toms*, which are the kings of any marble bag, and they all have exotic names such as Blood Royals, Rainbow Pearls, Ghost Lasers and Tom Birdcages. "At the start of the game," says one player in Melbourne, "you arrange who goes first and make all the rules. Like you decide if the marble can rebound off rocks and if you're allowed to buzz it by making a little dust storm instead of just rolling it. Then you make a hollow in the ground and try to get a marble in it. Once you've got a marble in the hole, you get a free shot and try to knock the other person's marbles. If you hit them, you win the marble."

Girls will be girls...sometimes

A FISTFUL OF DOLLS: Amy with her Barbie. £260 million worth are sold every year.

ON THE BALL: The same Amy. Girls demand the freedom to play whatever they like.

All for one and one for all...

PLAY is the best teacher of all. It teaches pulling together in a team, as when these children play ball in an African sunset. It teaches work, as when this boy potter in Colombia, South America (left) uses the skills he learnt in play to contribute to the adult world of

business and helps to pay for the next meal. And it teaches how the world works, as when this young girl in Africa (right) learns that a flat wheel when stood on end will roll and can be chased. All good lessons, all good games...and all good fun, too.

...as play begins to work

In the market for a good read – and time to take a letter

JUST a jumble of patterns on a page, but it doesn't mean a lot. That is until you start looking into it more closely. And in Chinese and Indian scripts, that can be a slow business, as these children below are just beginning to discover.

All pull together

LOOK, JUST HANDS: Tug of war doesn't even need a rope if you really put your mind to it.

ON TOW: Simeon is the outboard motor as older helps younger on a family holiday .

Master builders

CHARIOTS OF WIRE: An African DIY job.

'SOMETIMES I think at night that there's aliens who are about the size of my Lego men *{says Craig, above}* and they can sort of sink through the plastic and have a look inside and try pressing the buttons. They all come from a universe called Caprikus and when I take the model to bits later, I pretend that I hear someone saying: 'I've lost you...'

CHAPTER SIX: TALENTED CHILDREN

WEI CHUN: THE POLE STAR

'Before I go on stage I am nervous and my heart beats very fast. But as soon as I start to perform I relax'

Shanghai
CHINA

MORNING SCHOOL for Wei Chun consists largely of standing on a pole-vaulter's pole balanced horizontally on the shoulders of two strong men, bouncing up and down and doing backward somersaults.

An unusual education, but the fragile-looking Wei Chun is an unusual girl. At 12 she is one of the most promising young stars of the Shanghai Acrobatic Troupe. Her role is to perform one trick. One simple trick. One daring, spectacular, unforgettable, breath-taking trick. And it is just that – to bounce high in the air off the pole, do a backward somersault and land back on the pole; then to cap that by doing the same again, only this time with a *double* somersault thrown in. On stage, apart from all the waving and dancing and bowing and smiling that goes with it and the fancy cartwheel to get on the pole in the first place, the trick will take just a few dazzling seconds to perform. But learning how to do it has been Wei Chun's life for the past four years. That is why she stands this morning, like all the other mornings, on the pole in the school's gym, a tall barn of a building filled with ropes, boxes, harnesses, poles and straps. There Wei Chun is surrounded by the hubbub of all the other performers who are getting quietly on with practising their own tricks. Like the boy tossing a pile of bowls from his foot to his head and still dropping more than he catches. He will

PRACTICE: Wei Chun's life for the past four years.

PRACTICE: Strengthening exercises are all part of learning her trick.

do it thousands more times for years to come before they let him near a stage. And by then he will not drop any. Another girl is foot-juggling a large table. Others are spinning plates on the top of bamboo canes or practising arm swings on vertical poles. Two small girls are balancing on one hand and still more are just working out on strengthening exercises.

But Wei Chun sees none of this. All she sees is the pole and the men; all she hears is the voice of her trainer urging, correcting, encouraging, scolding her. The men move the pole up and down, and Wei Chun bounces as though she were on a trampoline, higher and higher until finally she flips over and lands, sure-footed, back on the pole. But it is not sure-footed enough for her trainer. He frowns as he helps her down and shows her how she should have kept her body in a straighter line. Wei Chun has hurt her arm and rubs it without any expression of pain as he talks to her. Then she is back on the pole and off they go all over again. The quest for perfection is relentless. Wei Chun takes criticism like a true professional: "Sometimes I make mistakes. Then I have to think hard about the reason for the mistake, so that I perform better the next time."

Wei Chun's is really a five-person act. She has two full-time trainers who stay with her throughout her years of learning, as do the young men who hold the pole. They are growing bigger and stronger as Wei Chun gets older and heavier, their weight adjusting to hers, constantly in tune with each other. For the training to work their relationship has to become almost intimate.

In the early days Wei Chun wore a harness to practise the somersaults in safety. One of her trainers, Wang Xi Gi, tells how he builds up the young gymnasts' confidence: "First I explain to them the dangers they will face. Then I make sure that they grasp the idea of the trick. This way the children can concentrate on their training. Then I tell them not to be nervous. They should relax. The more relaxed they are the less they fall. The more they worry about falling the more

READY: *Wei Chun prepares for her jump.*   **UP:** *Half-way through the somersault.*

OVER: A blur of red as Wei Chun spins.

DOWN: A safe landing – she's done it!

they fall. I also tell them about safety measures. This means the children must all work together and help each other. After getting over their initial fear they can go on with their training with full confidence."

Every day Wei Chun carries out exactly the same sequence of exercises in exactly the same order, the order they will finally be performed on stage. There are twenty-five separate actions in every set of exercises and as each is completed it is marked off in chalk on a bench. Nothing, but nothing, is left to chance.

And that is how it is six days a week, eleven months a year. Wei Chun's day begins before seven with warming-up exercises. All the children need at least three years' intensive training before they are considered ready to make their debut in the acrobatic theatre. Every day, before starting work on their own specialist trick, they go through the same basic training routine, designed to strengthen their bodies and develop their balance and coordination. Then it's time for breakfast, which Wei Chun takes with the others in the canteen. After that they go back to the gym by eight to start training proper. That is when the real work begins and Wei Chun climbs on to her pole. Morning training finishes at 11.30 and all the children head back to the canteen for bowls of lunch at large, circular tables. After a short nap it is time for lessons.

The acrobatic training school is managed by the State and must also provide a normal Chinese education. But these children are very privileged. They have just twelve to a class, while most Chinese children are taught in classes of fifty. In the afternoon there are four forty-five minute lessons, and then it is dinner. And in the evening she goes back for more training exercises. Wei Chun gets little or no free time until she troops back to the dormitory she shares with the other young girls. Her bed is a hard, metal, bottom bunk which she has draped around three sides with pastel-coloured material to soften it. Above the bed is a poster of a famous ballerina...Wei Chun dreams of being a star one day too. But for now her teddy is waiting and Wei Chun snuggles down to sleep.

It is a life full of long, hard days, but Wei Chun is one of the lucky ones. She lives close enough to the school to be able to go home every Sunday. That is the one day a week they have off. Some of her friends take two or three days to travel across the vastness of China to their homes, so they do not see their families too often. But they, like Wei Chun, have adapted.

"In the beginning," remembers Wei Chun, "when I first joined the acrobatic school, I always wanted my parents to stay longer after they brought me back. Sometimes my friends just started crying after their parents had gone. Now I'm used to it. Soon I'm going to tour Singapore for four days, but I am not going to miss my parents."

Yesterday was Sunday and Wei Chun was at home, helping her mother and her grandmother prepare the vegetables for the family's evening meal. She has always been close to her elder sister and they played together, giggling and joking as they did the washing up, bent over a bowl of soapy bubbles, playing with the foam, lifting it up high in the air and letting it fall through their fingers back into the bowl. Just another little girl in another Chinese family.

Life was as simple as that until Wei Chun was eight years old. She lived with her family and went to the local school. She had always been agile since she was tiny, so her parents were not surprised when she was chosen to take a gymnastics class at her primary school. Then one day a couple of years later Wei Chun saw a strange man standing at the back of the classroom, watching. She did not take much notice at the time. It was only when she was asked to stay behind after school that she discovered that the man was Mr Zheng from the acrobatic theatre. And Mr Zheng had found what he was looking for. A new star for a very special new trick. He was specifically looking for a girl to train for the newly-invented pole trick which was performed by only a very few throughout the whole of China.

He said later: "I needed to find a star person and to be this star the child had first of all to look good. This means her body and weight must be proportionate. It's good that Wei Chun is very slim. She must also have a good sense of balance when she is in the air. At the same time she must be in very good health. Then, if she trains hard, she should be able to come up to her teacher's expectations. We had all this in mind when we set out to search for someone like Wei Chun. But before we found her we looked at a lot of other children. None of them was ideal."

Wei Chun *was* ideal, but for her it meant the sudden end of normal childhood and family life. Once Wei Chun's family had accepted the offer that was being made, she had to leave behind all she had ever known and set off into a different world.

And now, four years after that day, Wei Chun is finally ready to perform her trick on stage in front of an audience. Four years is a long time to a twelve-year-old – one third of her lifetime. Four years of somersaults, of falls, of pain and boredom, work and exercise. Four years of getting up early, getting it right and getting it wrong, of praise and criticism, of off-days and finally of something very close to perfection.

And so one day Wei Chun finds herself sitting in front of a big mirror backstage at the theatre, the make-up before her, ready for the final transformation from little schoolgirl to grown-up artiste. This part is well-rehearsed.

"Before the performance I have to sort out my make-up and my shoes. At the beginning the teacher put the make-up on us. Now we have learnt to do it all ourselves, to make us look good on stage."

The practice trousers and sweater are swapped for a frilly tutu. Powder, rouge, lipstick and mascara follow, topped off with massive false eyelashes, popped right into place first go. She has obviously done that before, too. And there she is. The tiny girl, plucked from a primary school gym and honed and groomed and polished so thoroughly, is finally ready to be presented to the paying customers, including her parents and her sister in the front row.

In the theatre the music changes and Wei Chun runs out on to the big, red, circular mat, right into the spotlight as though she had been doing it all her life. She smiles the traditional gestures of the professional acrobat and then leaps up on to her pole. The first somersault is perfect and the audience roar their appreciation as she lands safely. Then it is time for the double and her two trainers creep in close, one on either side of the pole, just in case. Wei Chun bounces up and down, gently at first, then more strongly, higher and higher until the time is right. Then up and over and over and down. The trainers steady her landing. The audience adore her. Wei Chun bows and waves and beams.

But there is more. A young man runs forward and Wei Chun climbs on to his shoulders. Together they get back on the pole for the most difficult part of the trick. Total silence from the theatre audience. Gentle bounces, higher bounces, rolls of drums and a flash of two bodies arcing up through the lights as one, perfectly straight, down and back to the pole. Tumultuous applause goes on and on as Wei Chun and her partners bow and dance and laugh some more and then, almost reluctantly, Wei Chun backs off stage, still smiling and waving. Four years' work

NOVICE: The brilliant acrobat is a learner on roller skates with her big sister.

for that short time on stage...was it worth it? Just look at her smile. In a few minutes Wei Chun is Wei Chun again without the make-up, but still with the great big smile. She did it.

"I was nervous before I went on stage," she says. "My heart beat very fast. It went boom-boom. But when I started to perform I relaxed. It was a success."

Wei Chun is happy for another reason, too. Tomorrow is Sunday and she is going home for the day. Her sister has promised to take her roller skating in the park. Brilliant acrobat though she is, Wei Chun is still a novice skater, clutching on to her sister's hand and trying to get started. Would anyone who saw her first dazzling act, then chanced to walk through that park next day and come across this gawky, giggling girl wobbling around and trying desperately to keep her balance, believe that they were the same person – Wei Chun, the schoolgirl star of the Shanghai Acrobatic Show?

JULIO: THE SOCCER HOPEFUL

'I like playing on a large sunlit field, not being shut up in a classroom a long time. I get drowsy after lunch'

Rio
BRAZIL

IT IS A big day for Julio. The boy from the slums of Brazil, who has grown up lying awake at nights listening to the roar of the crowd at the mighty Maracana stadium down below in the city, has finally won himself a trial at the football club.

If he plays well, if he has the skill and ball-control, if the scouts like the look of him, if he seems strong and well-fed enough, if he has the stamina, if he's lucky...he may be called back for another trial later. And if that goes well too and if he can avoid injury and improve and do what the coaches tell him to do, then one day, one day a long way off, he just might end up playing for the famous Flamengo club at the Maracana, the biggest football stadium in the world.

It's a lot of ifs, but then Flamengo are not short of youngsters pleading for a trial. They look at more than 5,000 every year. They can afford to be choosy.

Ever since he was tiny, Julio has dreamed of being a great soccer star. Now at twelve years old he has his chance. Only a handful make it beyond that first game. But for those who do the rewards can be enormous. It is the difference between a life of riches, travelling the world, owning a big house, having enough to eat...or staying

JUGGLING: 'I must raise my head to improve.'

put in the favela slums of Rio and being hungry and poor. Only a game? Not for Julio, it isn't.

Home right now is a crude single-storey shack. The walls are built of rubble held together with cement. If you lean on one of them it wobbles and creaks. The whole of the inside is so small that it would easily fit into the lounge of an average British suburban semi. Julio shares this tiny hut with his mother, Cilea, brothers Bebeto, 18, and Alex, 8, and the mother's current boyfriend. There isn't much in the place, but they are proud to have a fridge, a stove and a television set. Julio has no illusions.

"We're poor, so we have a small house, but we like it very much. It used to be smaller and made of mud. Then my mother bought some bricks and made a bathroom and now there's enough room for everybody to sleep on the floor. We have mains water and pay for it, but it's no use – there's no water in the mains. So it's difficult. We have to wash the dishes outside. I fetch water, prepare food and wash the dishes. We wash with water from a bucket.On Sunday, my mum washes them.

"My mother used to work as a maid in someone's house. It was difficult to support the three of us. Now she works in a supermarket and it's easier. She leaves home at nine in the morning and returns at eight or nine in the evening. Sometimes she works overtime, and we manage as best we can.

"Sometimes I help her carry groceries back from where she works, when she gets paid. So I help her and she's very good to me. I really love her. She could have abandoned us when my father

SUNNY: 'Life has a good side and a bad side.'

abandoned us. She might have turned us out into the street to beg, but she didn't. She's so strong-willed. I have a good life, but it's a life divided into a good side and a bad side. The good part is playing, helping people, avoiding doing things wrong. The bad part is working all week only to be held up and robbed on pay day. It happened to my mother. That is hard – working the whole week, the whole month, and then being robbed."

Most of the year all three boys sleep on mattresses on the floor while their mother is on a shabby old sofa-bed. But when it rains the floor gets so damp that they all have to cram together on the bed. It is easy to see why Julio wants to get away, but his dream of football fame goes beyond poverty and riches. It is a dream of a young boy who wants to be a star like the heroes he watches. If only he can practise enough. Whenever he has the chance he is out with his friends on their dusty wasteground pitch. And several times a week he also plays for a local boys' club.

"My team is called Cantao and is made up of kids from a wide area. We train a lot, we practise penalty kicks. I'm a left winger. I like to do passes across the field, especially when I'm playing on a large or sunlit field. I like that. To be really good I need to keep a closer eye on the game, to raise my head more, be more conscious of my playing, hit the ball more. But I am improving."

Playing football isn't just a hobby for Julio. It's a passion. And it's the one thing he is really good at. School gives him few rewards.

"I don't like being shut up in a classroom a long time," he says. "And I get drowsy after lunch. I do like to play ball and other games."

But if he is not attentive, competent or enthusiastic inside the classroom, he is all those things out on the football pitch. Not that Julio is a show-off. He tries to ignore the spectators when he is playing, whether they are admirers or critics.

"Some people praise me a lot and think I'm an ace. Others think I've got no talent and others think that I'm middle of the road. But I don't take any notice, not of the good or the bad comments. It's true that I play both well and badly and everyone has the right to their own opinions."

Julio's inspiration comes from watching the real aces in action – the Flamengos down at the Maracana stadium. Whenever they can scrape the money together, Julio and his big brother Bebeto are there on the terraces. Fatherless Julio has a special attachment to his favourite idols.

"First there's Zico. He has a lot or experience, marks his opposite number well, doesn't foul other players, passes the ball well, is disciplined and breaks up fights. A lot of experience. I like Zico, my Zico. My other favourite is Roberto Dinamite. He's always joking – even when he misses a penalty."

To Julio these are real men, real success stories, offering real hope: "It's good to be a football player because it makes people happy. The crowds fill the stadium. They become involved in the game. The emotion makes them cry. There is a big emotional side of football with people milling around the changing room wanting your autograph, the press milling around."

When the day finally comes for his trial with Flamengo, Julio joins all the other boys on the training pitch and runs hard, tries his best, gives everything to that one all-important game of football. He plays well, but he fears not well enough.

"I felt I did well...but I missed a goal," he says sadly afterwards. "And I made certain other mistakes. I did OK, but I didn't play as well as usual. I was nervous with all those people around. I lacked a certain skill – I don't know why."

But Julio had done enough to impress the scouts. He was invited back to six more sessions with the Flamengo Junior Training Squad and got on well. But then the club moved their training ground right across to the other side of Rio and Julio could not afford the fares to get there. After moving so close to his dream of escaping from poverty, that very poverty kept him trapped. So instead, Julio is having to start thinking about a different kind of future. In a year's time he will have to leave school to earn some money to help his mother. Reality is taking the place of his dreams.

"When I grow up I want to be an engineer – doing construction work, designing buildings. I already draw quite well and that helps. If I had the choice I'd be a football player. So I might be a football player or an engineer. Or if neither of these work out then I might work in a supermarket."

TRIAL: 'I felt I did well, but I missed a goal. I didn't play as well as usual.'

DREAM: 'Football players make people happy...the emotion makes them cry.'

NIKHIL: BLIND CHESS PLAYER

'I like working on the computer and writing music. When I grow up maybe I'll get a job in the computer line. It's too early to say'

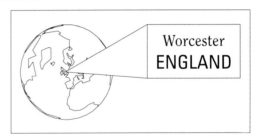

Worcester
ENGLAND

'MY NAME is Nikhil. I'm twelve years old and I go to Worcester College for the Blind in England. When I was about nine months old, I went with my family back to India for a holiday. I saw a doctor there and he thought I had a squint. But he thought it was a bit more than that. So I saw an eye specialist there and he found that I had an eye cancer called retina blastoma. So a few days after this discovery we came back to Britain. I went to a hospital here and had an operation to remove my right eye. I also had radiation treatment in my left eye. I carried on going to the hospital to have check-ups for a few years after that. But when I was about nine years old it was discovered that I had a cataract in my left eye which was a direct side-effect of the radiation. I had to have my left lens removed. For a while I had to wear glasses. Then I had some laser treatment – just to get rid of the fragments of the lens which were left and six months later I had a haemorrhage. A blood vessel burst and my retina soaked up the blood. So after that I haven't been able to see very much at all apart from light and dark.

Here at the school the boys are divided into three houses, literally, separate buildings with about thirteen to fifteen pupils in each and one or two house mothers who take it in turns to stay in the houses. It's like going home really after school, different people, not teachers at the houses. So you can get away from school so to speak. I go home to my family in London every three weeks or so. I think one of the main things I miss from home is the cooking really. I don't really get any Indian meals at school like I do at home.

In the College there's no set system about how to get around places. We've got to stick to the right of passages as much as possible to avoid collisions. I can find my way around inside all right. For stairs I use a counting system – only so I can get about them quickly. It isn't necessary in corridors and so on because I can tell by the doors. But it's outside that the problems start, once there's no walls or anything to follow. When I want to go over to the main building after school, say to tea or to practise piano or anything like that, I have first to go across the car park outside my house, which is normally all right. I find the garages and cut straight across till I find the main door. But occasionally there is a car in the way that I bump into.

I think I like maths best of all. That's one of my favourite subjects. And also keyboard skills, which is basically typing. I don't really enjoy the drama lesson. I don't know why, but I just don't enjoy it really.

I don't really like sport as such. But I do enjoy chess. For playing chess we've got specially adapted boards so that the black squares are raised and one of the colours has pins at the top so we can decipher the different pieces. The pieces have pins at the bottom which we fit into holes on the squares so that by feeling them we don't knock the pieces out of place. We can just feel the board and tell where the pieces are. I visualise where the pieces are a bit. One day I may be able to visualise the board completely but I can't at the moment. I feel it will be a while before I can do that.

I started playing the piano at the age of five and I played for about, oh, must have been six or seven years, by the Suzuki method. Now I'm playing by the conventional method, which means that I have to read the music, memorise it and then play it without actually hearing it on tape. Braille music is completely different from sighted music. It's like learning a different language rather than just an extension of English Braille. First there is a symbol for the pitch of the note, together with the length. In front of that you could have an octave sign instead of a stave, and after that you could have a fingering mark and before any of

COMPUTING: 'I remember when I could see pictures.'

this you may have a sharp or flat sign. And then after this you may have interval signs which are used for chords. It's slow to learn pieces, but I get quite a bit of satisfaction when I have.

I started playing brass a few years ago – I think it must have been about three years ago. For six months I played the euphonium and then I started learning to play the French horn. I spend a lot of time working on the computer. There's quite a range of things I can do. I enjoy word processing, writing music – all sorts of things, including creating graphics on the screen. I don't really know why I use graphics on the computer. I suppose I can remember the pictures from when I could actually see them, so I like to create them even now. I can still imagine the pictures quite well. As to how I actually make them...first I think of exactly what shape the picture is going to take on, then I think of it in terms of the graph, so to speak, of the computer screen. Then I type in the program actually to put it on the screen. But because I can't see the screen I need a bit of additional hardware – a voice-synthesiser which will read the screen together with the graphic software.

 I started learning to program in a language called BASIC. Then I went on to learn ASSEMBLER language which basically translates immediately into machine code and leads to fast programs. But a problem I have to face is that my voice synthesiser can't really pronounce

CHESSMAN: 'I do enjoy chess. One day I may be able to visualise the board completely.'

PIANIST: 'It's slow to learn pieces, but I get a lot of satisfaction when I have.'

the words, the mnemonics, of ASSEMBLER language very well, so I can't always understand what it's saying.

The most frustrating thing really is that you can't get the appropriate manuals for the computer in Braille, so my father usually has to read the manuals to me and I work from what I can remember.

I don't really know what I'll do when I grow up. I had some ideas about maybe getting a job in the computer line or something, but really it's too early to tell yet.

I don't really find I have a lot of problems relating to fully-sighted people. There's just one thing I find really difficult when I'm talking to someone and that's if they sound angry. I can't tell if they're really joking by the twinkle in their eye. I can't see their eye...

CHRISTINE: THE LINGUIST

'Greek is my favourite language, but I think and do my sums in English. It just depends what mood I'm in'

Brussels
BELGIUM

'MY NAME is Christine and I'm ten years old. I live in Brussels. My mother's Greek and my father's Northern Irish. I go to the European school which is a school with lots of language sections mixed – in fact all the languages of the European Community – English, French, German, Italian, Dutch and so on.

I was born in Greece, in Athens, and I lived there for about three years. Then I moved to England for a year. Nobody could understand Greek there – nobody we knew. So I went to playschool there and I had to learn English. When I was four we moved to Luxembourg. Then I spent afternoons at a day nursery where there were other Greek children. But at school in the morning I had to speak French, and on the streets and at shops. And I also learnt German at the school in Luxembourg as a second language, and that was about all until I was about six and a half. Then we moved to Brussels and I started going to the European school.

Sometimes I consider myself English – it depends what mood I'm in – sometimes Greek. At home I speak both English and Greek...it depends. When it's easier in English, I'll change to English. It's not that it's hard, that I can't speak Greek well, it's just that sometimes I can understand or speak better in English, sometimes in Greek. I don't really have a problem speaking English and Greek at home. But when my mum asks me a question, I've got to answer 'yes' or 'no'. And in Greek 'yes' is 'neh' but in English 'no' is 'no'. So when I shout it out whatever I say my mum doesn't know whether I'm saying 'no' in English or 'yes' in Greek. So she gets confused and gets the wrong message.

I do my sums in English most times, but sometimes in Greek. I learnt my times tables and everything in English. Sometimes I think in a different language, but mainly in English. English is really my first language. Greek, French and German are all second languages. I can speak a little bit of Italian and Dutch, too. I haven't picked up anything in Portuguese – too complicated I think. I can say a few words in Russian, though. My grandmother lived in Russia and so she sometimes speaks Russian at home. Like, for instance, "idi", which

HOPES: 'I speak four languages, but I would like to learn six one day.'

means "come here", or "dyengi" which means "money". But Greek is really my favourite language, because I speak it more than the others and I know it better, and that's the language I learnt first.

I think it's fun to learn lots of languages, but it depends on the teacher really. I mean, when I once had a strict teacher I didn't like it. Eventually I would like to learn more than four languages – maybe Italian or Spanish or something like that. I'll get the chance to learn one more language when I'm in my seventh year at school, and then later on one more still. That will mean I'll be able to speak six languages altogether.

SUNDAR: TEMPLE ARCHITECT

'When people see a temple, they praise the architect who created it without even knowing who he is. I love this praise'

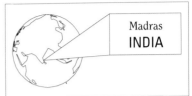

Madras
INDIA

'MY NAME is Sundar. I am 13 years old. I want to become a great temple architect. I have been interested in this profession since I was a very young boy. It is a family tradition. I study at the government College of Architecture which is quite close to the sea at Mahaballipuram, near Madras, India. My father studied here too. He has built a Bala Krishna temple at Chembur in Bombay. That's what made my father famous. Now he's working on a temple in Madras. It will take him at least seven years to complete the work. He specialises in stone carving. While I am studying here, I stay with my great-aunt. I normally get up at 6 o'clock in the morning. I brush my teeth and then sit down to study.

College starts at 8.30. The first three hours of the day are allotted to practical work – carving. I am very interested in that. At the moment we work in soapstone because we are very young. In the first year we will also get to carve in stone that is very soft. We will work with that in the second year too. In the third year, there is something called greenstone that we are given to work on. In the fourth year we have padaipukkal. As we progress on the course, so the stone gets harder and harder. At the moment we learn to make small flower designs. As we progress we will learn to make idols as such.

WORK: 'We make flower designs first, then idols.'

After practical work we have three lessons of theory. We are taught Sanskrit, iconography and iconometrics. It is important to learn Sanskrit because all the silpasastras are written in Sanskrit. Only when we can read these will we get to know the rules for making idols.

In the afternoon we have two more lessons in theory. Then the last two periods are for drawing. I like drawing very much. College finishes at 5 o'clock and I come back home. After washing, I have some free time. We have exams at the moment. For the exams we have forty-two hours to carve a piece. During exams I study very hard. I go back to study after dinner until

STUDY: 'We work in soapstone. As we progress the stone gets harder and harder.'

10 or 11 o'clock. I always study morning and evening on the roof outside. If I study downstairs there's a lot of noise but on the roof there is always a quiet atmosphere. I am a devout Hindu, like my father, and that's the inspiration for my work. I love working with stones. It's not just a desire to copy a design. I like to make something properly. I pray to God so that my sculpture may be perfect.

I don't want to build a temple just for the money I'll earn. When people view a temple they wonder about the person who created it. They praise the architect even without knowing who he is. I love this praise. That is why I very much want to be a temple architect.

RESULT: 'I don't want to build a temple just for the money .'

MIHO: THE MATHEMATICIAN

'I always practise definitely for three hours every weekday, six hours on Saturday and seven Sunday. But I sometimes finish early on Sunday'

Tokyo
JAPAN

MIHO Namura thinks Wednesday is the best day of the week because school finishes early. That means she can spend five whole hours in the evening doing sums. Addition, subtraction, multiplication and long division all night long as fast as she can.

And eleven-year-old Miho, who lives in Tokyo, Japan, the land of the calculator, does not use a single microchip to help her. Instead she does her sums on a soroban. A soroban is the Japanese version of the ancient Chinese abacus, a frame with rows of beads used for complex arithmetic. Despite the electronic revolution, led by Japan, the Japanese still use it as part of their daily life. Many shops, markets and railway stations rely on sorobans instead of pocket calculators or electronic cash tills to work out prices because...well, just because they'd rather. They've always done it that way. You can even buy a machine with a calculator on one side and a soroban on the other, though exactly why you'd want to no-one has quite worked out.

Fond as they are of tradition, the Japanese have become fanatical about this link with the past. It is taught in schools, and is said to build your character, and they hold massive competitions with regional heats and grand finals in huge halls to see who is the best soroban "player" in the country.

And Miho is one of the best, which is why she has to practise so hard. Not just on Wednesday evenings either.

"I practise every day," she says. "Monday, Tuesday, Thursday and Friday my elementary school finishes late. But I still always practise definitely for three hours. On Wednesday my practice can be longer, from four o'clock to nine o'clock. And on Saturday from three o'clock to nine o'clock. On Sunday it's from two o'clock until nine, or maybe even nine-thirty. But sometimes on Sunday I finish early."

Thirty hours' hard labour a week on top of normal school work and without any parental pressure is the sort of dedication not often found in an eleven-year-old. But Miho's nine-year-old brother Syun is at it too and doing his best to keep up with his smart sister. They both started learning the soroban when they were in a kindergarten run by an old friend of the family, Mr Kurakawa, who is still Miho's teacher .

Children in the kindergarten begin by doing lots of physical exercises to help their concentration. Even at this young age they each have their own individual soroban, which they keep in a little cloth case. They are taught to listen carefully as their teacher shouts out simple sums for them to do. All the time the children chant back the actions to their teacher: "thumb", "finger" and so on, until at the end the teacher asks if they have the answer. All the children raise their hands and shout: "Hai!" *{yes}*. The teacher calls on a child, who invariably gets the answer right, and all the children chorus: "Exactly!" and applaud.

Miho soon found that she wanted to do more with the soroban than she could in her normal

How the soroban works

IN ACTION: A youngster uses a soroban to calculate.

THE soroban is a wooden-framed instrument made up of 23 columns of beads, four below a dividing bar on each column and one above. Each column represents a unit of 10, so columns correspond to units, tens, hundreds, thousands and so on. Decimals can be calculated in the same way in the opposite direction (tenths, hundredths, thousandths and so on). The specific column that represents units on the soroban is a matter of choice, but once it is defined all other columns fall into place.

Each bead in the upper section above the dividing bar is equal to five times the unit value of its column when it is pushed down towards the bar (5, 50, 500, 5,000 and so on). If it is pushed up away from the bar, it is worth zero. Each of the four beads in the lower section is equal to the unit value of its column when it is pushed up towards the bar (1, 10, 100, 1,000 and so on) and zero when it is pushed down away from the bar.

By pushing different combinations of beads towards the dividing bar, it is possible to represent the numbers 0 to 9 on any single column. For example, if the upper bead is pushed down and all the lower four beads pushed up, the number 9 would be represented on that column. If the upper bead is pushed back up but the lower beads left in place, the number 4 would be represented on that column.

Numbers are put on to the soroban and then added a digit at a time. For example, the sum 123 + 456 would be done as follows. Firstly the 1 is entered on the hundreds column, followed by the 2 in the tens column and the 3 in the units. Next, the 4 is added to the 1, the 5 to the 2 and the 6 to the 3. At this point, the answer 579 appears on the soroban.

On the way through this one simple sum, the soroban reads first 000, then 100, 120, 123, 523, 573 and finally 579. The skill of the soroban player comes in making these simple single movements at lightning speed.

More complicated problems are solved in similar ways, working from left to right and computing a single digit at a time. Many Japanese find that they make fewer mistakes with a soroban than with a calculator, and it is not uncommon to see a shopkeeper use one to check his electronic till's answer.

ANZAN: Miho calculates without a soroban. Later she doesn't even move her fingers.

elementary school lessons and her teacher Mr Kurakawa recognised that she had a real talent. He felt that she was "something of a genius". So every day after school, Miho goes along to see Mr Kurakawa for extra work among a small group of equally-dedicated children.

Miho's parents are quite happy with her obsession. Both are very busy with their own careers as teachers in nearby schools. They simply want to give Miho and Syun every chance to do what they are interested in and are delighted that Miho is achieving such success in something that is so important to her. That Miho spends very little time at home does not seem to concern either her or her parents. She usually prefers to practise her soroban with Mr Kurakawa rather than alone in her little room at home, partly because whenever she tries to work there her pet budgerigar Peter insists on joining in, either by walking up her arm or trying to move the beads with his beak.

But the real point of all this seemingly pointless adding, subtracting, multiplying and dividing is the contests. Miho, an eleven-year-old who can beat most adults, is well used to being in competitions and is ready for the big one, the "All Tokyo". One day, she hopes she may even become the soroban champion of all Japan.

As she walks into the huge competition hall, several hundred other children are already arranging themselves at row after row of desks. Miho searches around until she finds her name on one of them and sits down. If she is nervous, she does not show it as she grins and chats to the girl beside her. Then out of her bag she fishes a stout wooden board and places it good and square on the desk in front of her, using sticky tape to fix it firmly in place. Next she takes out a blue velvet case, the sort you might expect to carry a musical instrument. Out of this comes the soroban, which she fits carefully on the board. Miho is ready to compete. As the opening

RIGHT: Miho holds up her answer ready to be checked.

PRIZE: Miho receives a trophy, a book and a certificate for her success.

ceremony begins, the conductor stands at the front with his helpers and reads out the competition instructions. Last year's champions hand back their flags and trophies ready to be won again and everyone claps loudly.

The hall goes quiet as the children wait, backs straight, ready for the off. Then suddenly the silence is broken by the conductor, shouting out a list of numbers as fast as he can, sounding for all the world like a tobacco auctioneer. The monotonous tone of his amplified voice is accompanied by hundreds of fingers clicking thousands of beads, up and down the sorobans. It sounds just like rain pattering on a tin roof. Some children quickly fall silent, unable to keep up with the machine-gun arithmetic being fired at them. They sit back, waiting for the rest to finish. But Miho and many others go on and on and on, getting the right answers faster than most of us could even write down the sums.

Then, as suddenly as it started, the voice stops. Miho scribbles her answer on a piece of paper and waves it in the air. One of the helpers comes down from the stage, checks it, tells her it is correct and hands it back to her. Miho, showing no emotion, waits for the next round.

But before it starts she pushes her soroban to one side and slumps forward on to the table, her head on her arm, looking as if she has given up and gone to sleep. There she stays, perfectly still, until the second barrage of arithmetic suddenly stops. Miho immediately looks up, moves some of the beads on her soroban, and writes on a piece of paper. Can she really have done that huge sum in her head? Miho waves her paper in the air as before and once again a helper comes down to confirm that her answer is correct.

This is the most remarkable soroban skill of all. It is called "anzan". Accomplished soroban players such as Miho find that they can gradually dispense with the physical rods and beads and simply imagine a soroban in their heads. Miho moves the imaginary beads around the imaginary soroban just as if she is working with the real thing – if not more quickly. It is incredible to watch, but it works. Not all the children in this competition have reached Miho's level of skill. Many are at an intermediate stage at which they still need to rely on some visible prompt to help them. They do not use the soroban, but they move their fingers up and down on the blank desk in front of them as though they were moving the imaginary beads which they picture in their heads.

On and on goes the contest for round after round and each time Miho finishes the calculations and holds up her piece of paper for checking without the slightest sign that she finds it in any way difficult or tiring. At last the final sum is done, the final answer checked and all the marks added up. The children wait calmly for the results and then the names are called. Miho is one of the very few to walk proudly up to the front and claim her prize – a trophy, a book and a certificate.

When it is over, Miho is warmly greeted by her father and her teacher, who always accompany her to competitions. She has come through the local and regional levels and must now prepare for the national competition. Miho is well on the way to her goal of being the best in Japan at what few outside Japan even know exists. It is not a skill that will be of much use to her in any other field. It might help a little in basic maths, but it will not make her a wizard mathematician. Playing a soroban is a skill that is mastered for the sake of that skill alone. That is enough for Miho and for the Japanese and they are happy to value and reward her.

CHAPTER SEVEN: MUSIC MAKERS

SHIHO AND NAO: VIOLINISTS

'My sister is always fooling around, but I don't fool around. I practise every day so that I make progress step by step'

Matsumoto
JAPAN

HOLDING a cigar box covered in white paper with a ruler stuck in one end and using a chopstick for a bow, Nao Kohno gets on with her violin lesson.

It doesn't sound wonderful. In fact it makes no sound at all, but two-year-old Nao is well on the way to being a proper player, just like her big sister Shiho.

Shiho is four and a seasoned violinist. She rolls off a list of the tunes she can play that is already bigger than she is.

"I practise many tunes," she says. "Butterfly; Christmas Song; A Mist Or A Cloud; Long, Long Ago; Allegro; Judo; A Joyful Morning; Etude; Minuette. I practise those at home a lot. All the time. My favourite piece is Long, Long Ago because it uses the third string."

The two sisters are surrounded by music from the moment they wake in the morning to their last lullaby at night and have been for as long as they can remember.

They are being taught music by the Suzuki method, named after a sprightly ninety-year-old called Sinichi Suzuki. He began to develop a way of teaching children music 50 years ago that involves constant saturation learning in which parents bombard their children with tapes, songs,

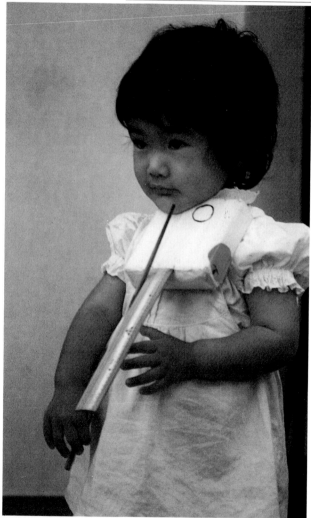

STARTING OUT: Nao and cigar-box violin.

instruments to play with, impromptu lessons, formal lessons, plenty of praise, and music, music, music.

Suzuki was first struck by how easily children learned the very difficult Japanese language from their mothers by picking up a little here, a little there, day after day after day until more and more stuck and the skill developed. If they can learn language that way, he reasoned, why

AT WORK: Shiho and Nao practise, but Nao soon gets tired and wanders off.

IN CONCERT: After all the work they are ready to perform in public.

not music? Before her children began learning, Mrs Kohno had never studied music, but now she is learning fast. She has to if she wants to keep up with her children. Their whole day is built around playing the violin. Recorded tapes are played over and over again as a model for and an accompaniment to their daily life. And then, at the appointed hour each day, their mother calls them to take out their violins. Practising for up to an hour each day, even for children so young, is not uncommon. Each new piece has been carefully selected to develop a particular aspect of playing position, tone and rhythm.

Ever since Shiho and Nao were born their lives have been filled with music like this. At first tapes and records of famous performances of violin concertos. Later recordings of the first tunes they were learning. Even while they are playing their normal childhood games, building with wooden bricks or looking at books, their lesson tapes are playing away in the background. Drip, drip, drip. This is learning by osmosis.

At two, Nao sometimes finds it difficult to fit in with all this rigid discipline and practice. By the time her big sister has taken her violin out of its case and the tape has begun, Nao has finished scraping away at her ruler and is rolling around the floor, kicking her legs in the air. It doesn't matter. Mrs Kohno knows that a little has rubbed off today, a little more to add to all the other little bits from all the other days.

Shiho is less forgiving.

"Nao is always fooling around," she complains. "I tell her that she mustn't practise because I want to practise. I don't fool around."

Shiho is a model Suzuki scholar. Her mother's smiles are reward enough for her, just like it says in the books that they should be. She knows that she has practised well. But Mrs Kohno also sticks a large red paper apple on the kitchen wall as a visible reward for progress. It sits next to a poster summarising the principles that govern childhood in the Kohno household. Shiho is already well on the way to knowing it by heart and she recites it like a prayer.

"I am practising every day some previous pieces by harmonising with tapes repeatedly. That is Suzuki method, which trains, educates children like us. I...I wish to complete rapidly new pieces of homework, one by one, to make progress step by step. This is Suzuki method which educates nicely children in Japan. I am one of the important pupils of our teacher."

Once a week Shiho and Nao are put into their best clothes and driven 50 miles by their mother to Suzuki's Talent Education Institute in Matsumoto City for a lesson with Mrs Mori.

Elaborate rituals surround the lessons in true Japanese style. The children bow to their teacher and then stand on sets of footprints that have been traced on sheets of card. This is to encourage them to stand correctly and still. Nao likes rolling on the floor and drawing on them, too.

First the children recite a haiku, a classic Japanese verse form, widely used in Suzuki for rhythm training. Nao has already learned much of it by heart and calls it out with gusto. Then it is time to start playing. Nao is first and she scrapes her chopstick across her ruler enthusiastically, imitating the movements she has seen made a thousand times by her sister, mother and teacher. It is soon too much for her and Nao looks around, loses her balance, falls on her bottom, giggles and wanders off. It doesn't matter. That's enough for one day. She'll get there.

Now it is Shiho's turn. By contrast to her sister, this four-year-old looks like a pro as she tucks her violin comfortably under her chin as though she were on a concert platform, waiting for her

ALL TOGETHER: 'My children are no more gifted than others,' says their mother.

cue from the conductor before launching into a concerto by Mendelssohn or Tschaikovsky. She plays her pieces and then is joined by two more little Suzuki pupils, boys no bigger than Shiho, but already well used to playing with her as a trio. They all begin exactly on cue as soon as Mrs Mori turns on the tape, chubby baby fingers working in unison. Mrs Mori moves around them adjusting the angle of an instrument here, altering the position of feet there, but the concentration is undisturbed. There is no hesitation, no faltering as they play *Twinkle, Twinkle* and *Gently Row*.

As Mrs Kohno takes her children home at the end of the lesson, she is still enthusiastic about the Suzuki method, even though it is such a big demand on her time.

"It is a wonderful system. It's not just a way of studying the violin, it's a way of bringing up children. My children play because they enjoy it. My aim is that they continue until they can play Mendelssohn's Violin Concerto."

The music leads to concerts, too, and after a few more months even Nao is ready to join in with a proper violin. After all the practice, they are ready to play at the national Suzuki concert in Tokyo itself. As the youngest players, their turn comes towards the end of the concert after the older children have played the A Minor Violin Concerto by Bach.

Then as the Master himself, Sinichi Suzuki, sits at the piano and plays the first bars of his theme song, Shiho and Nao, in the midst of a forest of dancing bows, play *Twinkle, Twinkle*. Not overawed by the occasion nor by the vastness of the hall in this huge city, far away from their small village, they drink in the occasion and the excitement. For them, it is just another part of growing up.

"I don't think my children are incredibly gifted," says Mrs Kohno. "There are plenty of other children more talented than they are. They just live in an enthusiastic and lively way."

DEWI: BALINESE DANCER

'I don't think I will ever stop dancing, it is a part of my life, but when I grow up I want to become a doctor like my sister'

BALI

REHEARSAL: The difficult movements.

DEWI is at the peak of her career as a dancer – at eleven years old. She is one of the leading exponents of the Legong, one of the stunningly beautiful and demanding classical dances that have made the tiny Indonesian island of Bali famous the world over. In a few years Dewi will be past her prime and will make way for younger dancers.

In Bali virtually every child is brought up in an artistic way as an expression of their Hindu faith. Just about everybody dances or plays in the gamelan, the village orchestra, or carves wood or stone, or paints, or arranges flowers, or makes dancing costumes.

"Balinese children, especially girls, always want to learn how to dance," says Dewi. "During the traditional ceremonies they are required to dance the sacred and entertainment dances. And dancing helps us to be at ease in human contacts. I started dancing when I was six. I practise twice a week, normally, each time for two hours. The dance I like the most is the Legong dance because there are many interesting and beautiful movements."

Dewi's mother was a famous Legong in her youth and has been her teacher since she was tiny. Now Dewi is one of the oldest and most accomplished in her mother's class, ready to dance the Legong in the temple along with her two friends, Tutuk and Koming. Ever since they were tiny these girls have been taught to move with incredible flexibility and precise control of every joint and muscle, from their necks to their fingertips and from their hips to their toes. They have learned to use their eyes to enchant the onlooker, darting them alarmingly from side to side. But one area where there is no room for flexibility is the choreography. The movements of the Legong are so exact that each has an individual name. At every training session Dewi's mother calls them out repeatedly while clapping out the complex rhythms and singing the accompaniment that is provided in

FLOWER: 'In every Balinese dance there is a religious side. We always pray.'

performance by the gamelan orchestra. She makes no concessions to anyone, not five-year-old novices nor eleven-year-old experts. Even the smallest girls are rigorously corrected. Each of their limbs and joints is pushed into perfect position over and over and over again until eventually their bodies dance the Legong automatically.

"Every day, other than dancing and going to school, I also help my mother cooking in the kitchen," says Dewi. "After the rice is cooked I make the Sesajen {*offerings*} to put in the family temple. Those offerings are for the ancestors and the last one I place on the ground is for the Butakala {*animal forces*}."

There are more religious festivals in the Balinese calendar than just about anywhere else in the world. And they are all strictly observed. All else, frequently including homework, must take second place. On a day when they are due to perform in the evening Dewi, Tutuk and Koming must spend much of the day preparing.

The make-up alone can take an hour and a half, skilfully applied by each girl's mother in the way that she was taught when she was herself a Legong. The look of the dancer's eyes is all-important, their natural beauty enhanced by a rich band of pink eye-shadow merging into mauve. Then the eyeline is strongly accentuated to balance the curve of the deeply blackened eyebrows. Red blushers and lips almost complete the picture, but not quite. Dewi's mother uses the stem of a frangipani flower to scrape up a white paste from the palm of her hand and make a triangle of white spots on each side of her daughter's face at the point where the forehead meets the temple. In former times the white paste would have been made from a special flour in the age-old traditional way. But progress has even reached the shores of Bali. Today Dewi's mother uses toothpaste and finds that it does the job just as well. Next she places one spot in between the eyebrows in the centre of a small black symbol of beauty in dancers, known as the Priasan. She makes identical marks on each girl and then, finally, heavily powders their faces – an essential protection against the sweltering tropical heat.

Dewi, Tutuk and Koming are now ready to get dressed in the Legong costume. It is made from the finest cloths, stitched by women from the village, embroidered with gold and finished with beads and semi-precious stones. The design is as ancient as the dance itself, though no one can trace its origins for sure. The Balinese have a special name for each detail and faithfully reproduce it for each generation of child dancers.

First they put on a wrapped skirt and and a tight-sleeved tunic. Dewi and Tutuk will play the principal roles in the drama, the 'Legongs', so their dress is green. Koming will play the assistant, the 'Tjongdong', so her dress is mauve. A skirt and tunic is more than enough for anyone to wear in the Balinese heat, even without dancing. But this is only the beginning. The 'Saboks' come next. These are long strips of fabric about four inches wide which are safety-pinned to the girls' waistbands and then bound tightly around their bodies all the way up to the armpits. Dewi jokes that she cannot move inside her cocoon. But that is just the point. She is not meant to. The idea is that by holding the dancer's torso rigid the incredible virtuosity of her limb movements are all the more striking.

There is still more to come. Each girl wears a belt around her waist, with an ornamental piece hanging down on each hip and another on her bottom. Then there is a long fringed sash running from the chest right down to the knees, plus vests and collars. Dewi and Tutuk wear stiff garments of red and gold, laced up at the front, while Koming's is made entirely from tiny beads. The only parts of the body that are left unadorned are the feet and the hands, except for the fans that the older girls carry.

Finally come the heavy gold helmets adorned with exotically perfumed sprays of frangipani, cream and yellow jasmine flowers, tipped with a hint of mauve. Early that morning Dewi and her friends had been out to collect a basket full of the most perfect flower heads they could find. Then they carefully spiked them on to dozens of wires that make up the centre of the helmet. Like the rest of the magnificent Legong costume, these helmets were designed for their beauty rather than the comfort of the wearer. Dewi closes her eyes and braces herself as her mother pushes her hair up inside the helmet and eases it tightly over her temples. Such discomforts are soon forgotten as the girls realise that the transformation is complete. Three stunningly beautiful

Legong dancers gaze admiringly at each other, hardly able to recognise their friends. For a few moments they stand serene, then they are off down the lane towards the temple. On the way, they relax enough to become young girls again and collapse in fits of giggles. Underneath it all they are still Dewi, Tutuk and Koming.

Meanwhile the festival preparations are well under way at the Temple. The heavy gong has been moved into position and all the instruments including the drums are being finely tuned. The gamelan is ready to play. Tourists may treat the Legong as a spectacle to be admired for its charm, beauty and skill, but the Balinese do not think of it in that way. At its root it is an act of religious devotion, an offering to the gods.

"In every Balinese dance there is a religious side," says Dewi. "We always pray and make offerings before dancing. This is to ask for protection and success so that the performance runs well."

As the three young dancers arrive the priest is already chanting and burning incense. He sacrifices a day-old chick, then sprinkles holy water over the girls' head-dresses. They are ready, their composure is perfect, their appearance serene.

The gongs begin to play and Koming, as the Tjondong, enters the circle alone and begins the dance. Then Dewi and Tutuk, the two Legongs, enter. The gamelan plays a more vigorous melody as the three dancers weave around in patterns of arms and fingers, heads and eyes. They begin to enact the ancient drama.

Dewi says: "The Legong dance tells the love story between the Princess Rangkesari and Raden Panji. The Princess is kidnapped by the arrogant King Prabulasem, who is waging war on her father."

There are several endings to the story, depending on which village is performing it. Most often Princess Rangkesari refuses to accept the King Prabulasem, even after he promises to give up the war. So Prabulasem sets off angrily to kill the Princess's father. Then there is a battle, but in the middle of it a blackbird flies in front of Prabulasem. This is a bad omen and he is killed.

The dance can last well over an hour with little respite for the girls, but they do not seem to find it tiring despite the heavy costume. But Dewi admits that she is not entirely confident about dancing the Legong.

"It has many different and difficult movements," she says. "For me the most difficult is the Bapangnya. When I know I have to dance this I always feel sort of afraid. But once this part is over I feel at ease. The communion of spirit between the music and the dance movements is very deep. But for me this is not difficult to achieve because ever since I was very small I have been listening to Balinese music and making it one with the movements."

Throughout the performance a small girl in the audience, little more than a toddler, has been standing transfixed by the dancers and copying the movements with tiny gestures of her chubby arms and wrists. This has been her first lesson in the dance that she too may be performing in a few years' time. Traditionally Legong dancers reached their peak at puberty, after which they would be married off, often to a high-caste suitor. Dewi has a more liberated view of her future. For one thing, she enjoys school, works hard and last year came top of the class. She wants to take advantage of the modern world without losing the values of Bali.

"When I grow up, I would like to become a doctor like my sister. But I don't think I will ever stop dancing, for dancing is already a part of my life."

GEDE: THE ORCHESTRA BOY

As a tiny baby he would copy his father, hammering on a block of wood with a stick. At six he played with the grown-ups

BALI

AT THE end of the day, Gede the duck boy can be seen shepherding a flock of waddling ducks down the narrow track past the temple that leads towards his home. Just like generations of small Balinese boys before him, he uses a white cloth on the end of a stick to guide them. Gede can often be seen out on the rice terraces after school, keeping an eye on the family's large flock of Indian Runner ducks. They keep the rice fields free of surplus grain and parasites.

Tending ducks is not the only tradition that Gede enjoys. He is also a fine musician, playing in the village gamelan orchestra when Dewi, Tutuk and Koming dance the Legong. Normally Gede is quiet and shy, but when he plays music he comes to life. He is only ten years old, but for four of those years he has been a member of the gamelan. Anywhere else that would be a remarkable achievement. But in Bali children learn to play the gamelan and dance before they can walk. In playing the gamelan, as in herding the ducks, Gede is simply following his ancestors. He is already a highly accomplished player, just like his father and grandfather.

The main instruments in the gamelan orchestra are gongs of all shapes and sizes. Gede's instrument looks a cross between a glockenspiel and a xylophone. It consists of ten metal bars mounted on an ornately carved base of red and gold. Gede strikes the notes with what looks like a carpenter's hammer, except that one end of the head is viciously pointed. He uses his left hand to dampen each note two notes after he struck it – an amazing feat of coordination.

The tuning of the instrument is precise and distinctively Balinese. The notes and rhythms sound exotically unfamiliar to anyone brought up on Western music. But these scales are no problem for Gede. His ears have been tuned to them since he was a tiny baby, listening and watching whenever the gamelan was playing. He used to imitate his father and grandfather, hammering with a stick on a block of wood. Later he sat between his father's legs as he practised. Eventually Gede was allowed to hold the hammer himself, while his father guided the boy's small hand to pick out one of the main tunes of the gamelan.

From that moment there was no stopping Gede. He practised those complex patterns over and over until he mastered them. But Gede was not just learning an instrument for the sake of it. He was becoming a part of the religious and spiritual life of the island. Already for each village festival he takes his place alongside all the other gongs, the drums and the cymbals. Each has a different part to play, the rhythms are complex, overlapping and superimposed on top of one another. Gede's skill lies not only in mastering his own part, but in being tuned in almost instinctively to the other players – his father, cousins and friends.

Remarkably, there is no conductor. One of the hand-drummers who sits cross-legged at the front is leader. His drumming signals to Gede when to change the pace of his playing, when to become more intense and when to quieten, but like all the players Gede's attention is mainly on the dancers, matching his sounds to their intricate gestures, leading them as he leads his ducks, just like so many of his forefathers have done.

FLOCKING IN: Gede looks after the family's flock of ducks.

TUNING IN: Every note is dampened with the left hand after it is played.

TSHACA: THE MBIRA MAESTRO

'At first I made a lot of mistakes. I felt I was playing badly. I practised, then on the third day I started doing very well'

ZIMBABWE

TSHACA fell in love with the strange-looking karimba mbira the moment he set eyes on it, and he knew right away that he wanted to learn to play it. The mbira, or "thumb piano" as it is known, almost hides the player behind a huge black-lacquered calabash that resonates the sound. Inside the player plucks a line of twenty metal keys with his thumbs and right index finger only. Bottle tops loosely wired around the top of the calabash add a buzzing quality to the metallic harp-like sound.

"I first saw the mbira when I came to school in 1983," says Tshaca. "I saw others learning to play and asked them to give me a try. I liked it, so I went to our teacher, Mr Chawasarira, and asked him to teach me how to play. He showed me how – he would say: 'Play this key' and I would try to play it. At first I made lots of mistakes. I felt I was playing badly. So he gave me the mbira and said I should take it home to practise and then come back and tell him how well I had done.

STAR: 'This boy is really talented.'

"I took it home for two days. Then when I came back to school on the third day I started doing very well. I practised every song he composed for us to play, until eventually I could play as well as I am able to now."

Today, 12-year-old Tshaca plays his own songs and even makes his own mbiras.

"I start by selecting wood for the base of the mbira and splitting it into two halves. It has to be a certain kind of wood that will not crack.

"I take the better half and carve this into a flat platform on which the mbira keys will sit. Then I hammer metal wire into the shape required for the keys. I start hitting the wire so that it becomes flat, then I file and hammer the sides to get the right tone. Then I have to make them smooth so they won't scratch my hands. So I get a stone to grind them.

"Then I fix the bridge by making about five holes in the platform and tying it on properly so when I fit the keys into position they won't come off. I work on each of the keys until they are in tune. Then I use burnt bottle tops to fit on the calabash to make the sound box. When all this is done I am ready to start playing my mbira."

"Africa, Africa..." he sings, sitting in the cooking area of the compound in the dusty, cattle-grazing grasslands of rural Zimbabwe at the end of the day. It is one of his own songs.

Tshaca owes his love for the mbira to his teacher's infectious enthusiasm for reviving traditional African instruments that were virtually suppressed when the country was under white domination. As headteacher of tiny Zingea Primary School, Mr Chawasarira has a captive group of young pupils, who love making music, singing and dancing.

Mystery still surrounds Tshaca's background. He has lost his parents and now lives with his uncle, who works as a patrol man on the widely dispersed farm, shepherding cattle that stray,

KEEN: Tshaca and Mr Chawasarira: 'I asked to try.'

protected only by the bow and arrows slung over his shoulder. Tshaca's uncle is rarely at home in their remote mud dwelling. Tshaca did not have much of a family life until he went to Mr Chawasarira's school. In the mbira he has found a skill that gives him satisfaction and recognition. And in Mr Chawasarira he has found not just a teacher, but a father-figure. Their relationship is close, warm and humorous, strengthened by the fact that Mr Chawasarira has no sons of his own. It is not surprising that Tshaca's ambition is to become a teacher of traditional music himself. Nor is it surprising to hear Mr Chawasarira's unhesitating confirmation of Tshaca's potential as an mbira player.

"I've found a special talent in Tshaca. I taught him the basics and he mastered them on the very same day. I was very happy to find such a boy. So I offered him an mbira to take home and learn some more. The following day he came and he had mastered even the variations – variations 1 and 2, so I had to add more variations for him. Within a week he had mastered nearly five variations. Then I thought – well, this boy is really talented. He shows great interest in the instrument. He's also getting into the tuning pattern. He can tune an mbira very well. You see, he's even tried to make his own mbira at home. He's brought it to me, and played it over to me."

Tshaca's playing can soon begin to sound repetitive, especially as Tshaca and his friends are happy to go on playing the same piece for hours and hours and hours. Tshaca's kind of music is built on cyclical patterns of sound. His task is to work together with the drummers and other mbira players generating a constantly changing kaleidoscope of variations on the basic theme. His skill lies in coordinating a series of complex rhythm patterns that on the face of it can seem to be in opposition. Much of the challenge in becoming a master of the mbira lies in being able to tune in to what each of the other players is doing, and adding to the development of the whole. Tshaca and his friends go on and on until they have exhausted all the possibilities in a particular cycle of themes.

It takes a lot of endurance to play like that and there can be technical difficulties with sustained playing, especially when the sun is high in the sky, as Tshaca explains: "When playing the mbira in full sun it can happen that the drummer may lose the pace because the sun is holding back the mbira sound. The mbira playing will be at a slower speed and the sound of the keys will have been messed up so that you will end up playing a different tune. So, when there is too much sun, playing the mbira well is difficult."

The mbira is also believed to have special powers to liberate anyone possessed by an evil spirit, and traditionally an accomplished mbira player like Tshaca would serve an important healing function in the village.

"The sick person goes to the 'Nango' as he is called and he tries to find the cause of the illness," says Mr Chawasarira. "He or she is told about the spirit that would like to possess him, but the spirit must be got rid of and the only person that can call that spirit is the mbira player. The spirit is only called by the music made on the mbira and nothing else. So the sick person goes home and they call in the mbira player. Then he plays to try to call out the spirit and he finds that the spirits come – the person who has been ill wakes up dispossessed and starts dancing very strongly. It is very peculiar the way it happens, but I have seen it with my own eyes and I have experienced the mbira playing. You find if the mbira is played throughout the night, the following morning the sick person is all right."

The healing powers of the mbira are not in much demand nowadays. But Tshaca and his friends are much in demand to play and sing at local festivals and celebrations, especially the Africa Day organised each year for the whole farm community. The musicians are rewarded with crates of locally-produced Fanta and Coca-cola and their elders enjoy pails foaming over with still-fermenting millet beer. Then it is the turn of the dancers to entertain, led by Mr Chawasarira's eight-year-old daughter, Dadirai. She is soon leading everyone – young and old, men, women and children. Divisions between performers and audience do not apply here. The urge to express the rhythms through movement and dance is irresistible. Tshaca moves with the music almost as much as the dancers. As the rhythm flows through the long line of calabashes, he knows that he will still be playing his mbira long after the sun has gone down.

AFRICA DAY: 'It is hard playing when there is too much sun.'

REHEARSAL: 'I practise every song composed for us until I can play it well.'

CECILIA: THE SINGER

'I practise with my two school friends, a contralto and a mezzo-soprano. It is a great deal of work, but after a concert there is loud applause and it is nice'

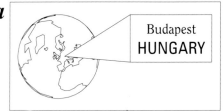

Budapest
HUNGARY

TWELVE-YEAR-OLD Cecilia picks up a new music book, sings a tune she has never heard before, then plays it on her violin. Her brother Bence, 11, and nine-year-old Dani join in and accompany her on cello and piano. They have never heard the tune before, either.

Mr and Mrs Bucsi do not think that there is anything exceptional about this. They do not believe their children are unusually gifted. They expect that all their children will be able to sight-read music just as easily as they will read a story book by the end of primary school.

The family live just below the Castle Hill in central Budapest, the capital of Hungary. Mostly they play together, but sometimes they play different pieces at the same time. The neighbours are well used to the effect of this. It just means that the five Bucsi children are practising again. In Hungary, more and more children are being brought up like the Bucsi family, in a deliberately musical atmosphere both at home and especially at school. Hungarian primary schools are organised to place special emphasis on teaching music, as well as teaching through music.

It is largely due to the influence of one man, the composer and musician Zoltan Kodaly. He was appalled by the poor standard of music teaching in the nation's schools. He wrote in 1929: "The greatest trouble is not the emptiness of the purse, but the emptiness of the soul, and of this we have more than our share. A vast area of Hungarian children's soul is a wasteland today. Singing is the Cinderella among school subjects, but the Prince will come to fetch her – the shoe will only fit her foot. We must lead great masses to music. An instrumental culture can never be a culture of masses. What is the violin or piano to you? You have an instrument in your throat with a more beautiful tone than any violin in the world if you will only use it."

Cecilia's father was one of the first generation of children to benefit from Kodaly's vision at the first musical primary school in 1945. Now his children are following him.

"I have three younger brothers and a sister," says Cecilia. "The oldest of my brothers is Bence in the fifth form, then comes Dani who is in the fourth form. Levente has just gone to the first form and enjoys school a lot. He goes to the Zoltan Kodaly Choir School. Sophie is still in kindergarten. Well, when the family is together we normally sing folk songs, guitar songs for young people and children's songs.

"Levente and Sophie were three when they started to go to the music kindergarten of Kati Forrai. They liked it very much. Levente often performed in the music kindergarten and Aunt Kati always praises him. Sophie is a little bit shy but she also likes to sing very much. I also went to the music kindergarten at the age of three.

"When the children go into the kindergarten, everybody sings out his or her name. Then Aunt Kati plays the flute or sings and the children have to indicate with their hands whether they have heard low or high notes. After that they sing. In the first year children learn the basic things. They have to differentiate between low and high notes, and later learn solmization {doh-ray-me} before they leave the kindergarten. The children have a knowledge of music, using the Kodaly method, by the time they go to school. I mean, solmization and clapping the rhythm. Aunt Kati teaches that music is close to the heart, and that you have to play music with all your heart."

Cecilia went from music kindergarten to music primary school and at the age of eight she was accepted into the prestigious Jubilate children's choir. Now, four years later, she is getting her first experience of a big concert

FAMILY FAVOURITES: Cecilia with Bence and Dani.

at the National Academy of Music where Kodaly himself worked. "We have been preparing for the concert for several months. The way we prepare is called 'repetition'. I practise with two of my school friends, Balazs, who sings the contralto part, and Eszter, the mezzo-soprano. We practise together until we feel we can sing the piece very well. Then we repeat it for our teacher, Ferenc Sapszon. He is the leader and main founder of the choir school and the choir. He has been the director for about ten years. When Mr Sapszon thinks we can sing the piece well enough we are allowed to perform at a concert.

"He spends a lot of time with the choir, as much as six hours a week or even more when we have a vacation. For example, he taught us *The Night* part by part and each of us had to sing his or her own part separately, then rehearse the parts together, then three parts until the whole piece was built up slowly. It is a great deal of work because we had to sing in tune and there are really unusual figures in the piece and we had to rehearse in pairs, then sing five to six parts together.

"We sang at the concert Singing Youth. It was held at the Ferenc Listz Academy of Music. It has a small and a large concert hall and major musicians of the future are trained there. Most of the audience were family members but choirmasters and music experts were there too. My father and my eldest brother Bence were there and liked it very much.

"At first we sang the Galus Domina and Kodaly's Invocation to get our voices ready for the required pitch. Then we performed the most difficult piece, *The Night*. I think it was very successful, the best performance I have ever given with the choir. We were a bit nervous before the concert. But afterwards we felt it had been very successful because there was loud applause and it was nice. I think the composer wanted to express the shiver you feel when, for example, you go out into the darkness where frightening creatures appear in front of you – bats and birds are flying and the trees and wind are whistling."

KYLE: THE SWORD DANCER

'I don't like competitions because if you don't get a medal you feel sort of sad. I like entertaining at Highland nights'

Aberfeldy
SCOTLAND

STYLE: 'Often my mind wanders.'

'MY NAME is Kyle. I come from Aberfeldy in Central Scotland and I'm 11 years old. I live on a farm with my Dad, my Mother and my brother Gavin. We have five dogs and nine hundred sheep.

I've been dancing since I was four years old. I started in dancing because I had "clicky hips". They were dislocated and I had to be in plaster for eighteen months. My legs were very weak. My mother says they were as thin as matchsticks. The dancing helped to build up the muscles. And I like the music.

I've been practising in the barn a lot lately, getting ready to enter the Sword Dance competition at the Pitlochry Games. The adjudicators are looking for toes pointed and arms in the correct positions. My weak point is getting up on my toes.

The history of the Sword Dance is that the soldiers, before they went off to battle, they used to dance across their swords. If they touched a sword it meant they would die the next day. I once did that at a competition in Dundee. I was dancing around and you're supposed to go back to the hilt of the sword and I went round too far. I got all muddled up and went and kicked the sword. It went flying across the stage. I just had to stand there until the dance had finished. When you've got your costume on it's really heavy with the kilt, the belt and the sporran. You have to work harder to jump up. It feels like you've got a ton on you. It's quite hard in the open competition, in the group I'm in. I was a bit nervous. I stop concentrating sometimes. My mind wanders away or sometimes I'm thinking about something different. I just forget a step. Or sometimes it's silliness.

I came third in the competition, so I got a bronze medal. But I don't really like competitions because if you don't get a medal you feel sort of sad. But I like entertaining people at Ceilis and Highland nights. I wouldn't want to do any other kind of dancing.'

CHAPTER EIGHT: BELIEF

DIAS: THE BOY MONK

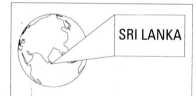

SRI LANKA

'I like all parts of our daily life, especially begging for alms. Till I die I will remain a monk'

DIAS the monk has just six and a half hours sleep a night and one small meal a day. He spends nearly all those waking hours working, cleaning and sweeping, praying or studying, with very little time to himself. When he gets hungry all he is allowed is a cup of tea. When he is tired he chants his holy texts more loudly to keep himself awake. Dias is just eleven years old. But there is not a hint of complaint in his voice as he talks about those long days.

"I get up at five o'clock in the morning when the bell wakes me, wash my mouth, drink a little water and start reading my books. When the bell rings again, I wash my face and then help with sweeping and cleaning and tidying, until the bell at six thirty tells us to go to the Shrine room and pray. After prayers we have our morning tea. At eight o'clock I start my lessons, learning and reciting what I have been given. Then I am free to do whatever is needed until eleven when we take our begging bowl and walk in a long line to receive our meal. We come back to eat our lunch.

"When the bell rings again I go into a corner on my own and recite the scriptures very loudly so that I don't get drowsy. All the priests do the same – it makes a lot of noise. At one o'clock we go to school and a teacher from the college gives us our lessons. We learn six subjects: Mathematics, English, Pali, Sanskrit, Sinhala and Tripitake, which is religion.

"We have a break for tea in the middle of the afternoon and then work on until the bell at five-thirty when we help with the sweeping. At nine o'clock we go to the Temple for the service,

ROBES: 'My mother was happy for me.'

TOLL: Each bell has a message.

where we worship and say prayers. Then we're free to rest until seven-thirty. There's no meal in the evening, just a drink of tea or coriander water. Then we go again into our own little corners and think about what we have done in the day, and revise everything. I like all the parts of our daily life, especially begging for alms.

"At nine o'clock we have some more tea and get our things ready for the next day. At ten-thirty the bell rings three times which means that we can go to sleep."

A severe, unrelenting life for a little boy, but it is borne with an acceptance handed down by generations of his forefathers who have followed the belief of Buddhism. It is an acceptance which equally stops a boy of eleven complaining of hunger and lets him leave his family in their mountain village with hardly a tear in his eye. And it is the same acceptance which helps his mother let him go.

Dias recalls: "One day at the Galle Temple a head-priest said to me: 'Would you like to become a priest?' I said: 'Well, I would.'

"Then the priest told me: 'Go and get permission from your mother, then come back and let me know.' So I came back and asked my mother. She was agreeable. I returned to the priest and told him that my mother was very happy about my becoming a priest. The chief priest started to organise my ordination."

Dias's family are both proud and excited at his chance. To be accepted into the Buddhist monastic order will ensure him a good education, high status and the important role of a monk. It will also mean leaving his family for good in their mountain village and travelling ninety miles to the Temple of Kesbewa in Colombo. He will hardly ever see them again.

The preparations do not take long. A monk makes the robes which Dias will wear instead of his everyday clothes. Dias has lessons in the chants and texts of his new life and the morning of his departure soon arrives. Dias is excited. He dresses in a white shirt and white shorts and is surrounded by all the children of his large family. His mother prepares a special meal for the whole family. It is special for her, too. It is the last that she will ever make for her young son.

"We had a morning meal at my aunt's house," says Dias. "My uncle, aunt and their children were there, and also my mother, sisters and brother."

The table is full of delicacies, foods that they do not normally have, to mark off this day as important and special. Dias lights some incense to begin the meal, then his mother takes some cake and pops it into Dias's mouth. If he is thinking at all about the fact that this is his last family meal, his last meal where he will eat anything but the most simple of foods, his last meal where he will have any choice about what he eats, then it does not show on his face. The tears are in his mother's eyes.

The meal over, it is time for Dias to say a ceremonial goodbye to his family.

He bends low at his aunt's feet, his hands together in front of his face. Then he moves steadily around the family circle, offering his final farewells as a son, a grandson, a nephew and a brother. Finally his younger brothers and sisters prostrate themselves at his feet. The brother they have always played with must now be treated with respect.

WORK: There is always water to be carried.

"Even as a boy leaving for school in the morning I used to show my respect to my mother and father and all the elders in the family," he says.

Then the minibus arrives to take him and his mother to the Temple. As he stands with his mother waiting for the final moment of departure, he gives her a small gift and it all becomes too much. He at last has to wipe the back of his hand across his eyes. Dias's mother tells him: "May you have the blessing of Buddha, Dhama and Sangha for success in your ordained life."

Then they are off. The family watch and wave until the bus is so small that they can no longer see his tiny hand waving from the window. Dias's journey has begun. He is not yet a monk, but already he is no longer a son.

When Dias and the other boys who are to be ordained arrive at the Temple, trumpeters and drummers in ornate dress are already dancing and playing loudly. Dias is led over to a line of monks with his mother beside him. He cups one hand and his mother solemnly pours a little oil into his palm as a symbolic gesture to show that she is now ready to hand over her son to the monks.

Then it is time for Dias the boy to be transformed into Dias the monk. A young monk begins to shave his head with great care and gentleness, pausing to place a little of the black hair into Dias's palm. "A little bit of hair was cut," he recalls later. "I was told to keep it and then I went to bathe and I don't know what happened to it after that."

Dias's mother looks on. "I was sad when they shaved his head," she says later. "I could remember his childhood and his playful times. I felt sad and turned aside to the Bo tree and kept

ORDINATION: A young monk starts to shave the hair from Dias's head.

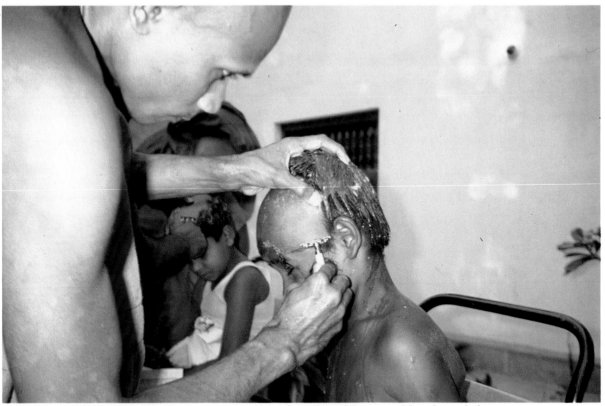

CLOSE: 'A little bit of hair was put into my hand and I was told to keep it.'

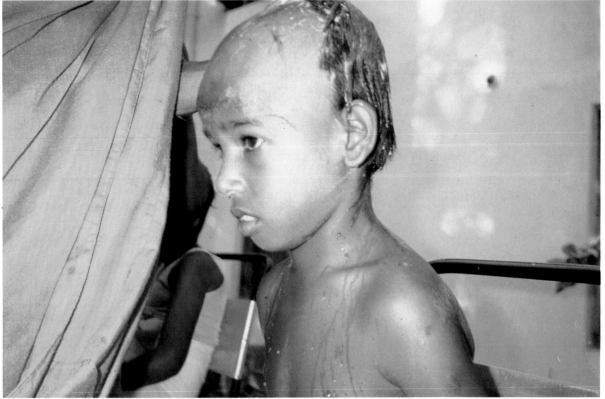

CLOSER: 'I was sad when they shaved him,' says his mother.

WHAT IS BUDDHISM?

BUDDHISM is based on the teachings of The Buddha, a prince called Guatama Siddhartha, who was born on the borders of modern-day India and Nepal in 563 BC. He married a princess, had three palaces to live in and vast wealth but, just as his son was born, he gave it all away in the Great Renunciation so that he could go in search of the Truth.

Great men taught him all they knew, he faced temptation from Mara the devil, but finally he found true Enlightenment and Awakening. He devoted the rest of his life to trying to pass on the Way to Enlightenment – the Four Noble Truths and the Eightfold Path to Awakening.

Since his death in 483 BC the practice of Buddhism has spread all over the world, through India and Sri Lanka, Tibet and to Japan and the West. Buddhism is more of a way of life than a religion. No gods or idols are worshipped. No war has ever been fought or opponent tortured in its name. Buddhism teaches that suffering is a basic experience in a human's life and that the cause of that suffering is man's constant selfish desire which keeps him in a permanent state of want, or of fear of losing what he has. If man can remove that underlying condition of desire then he need no longer be dominated by it but can experience freedom.

Buddhist monks try to eliminate the causes of desire through devotion, discipline and detachment. In this way, they believe they can put the needs of their fellow men before their own selfish concerns. Thus they will serve the world better and at the same time find their own salvation.

looking away. But then I recovered and rejoiced at the future well-being of my son, even though he has to be away from us."

All around the Temple the same thing is happening to the other little boys who arrived at the same time. And as their heads become bare it is already difficult to tell one from another. They no longer stand out as distinctly individual children, but are starting to look like miniature versions of the older monks around them.

More is to come. The boys' heads are wrapped in white turbans and they are led into the Temple, each one holding the hand of the monk who shaved him. Their feet are washed and they are taken to sit cross-legged on rugs in front of the chief monk. Their mothers sit in the Temple and watch. When it is Dias's turn to be ordained, the oldest monk chants and Dias echoes the same long sentences, only faltering once or twice.

"I take the teaching of Buddha as my refuge. I undertake to abstain from harming life. Venerable sir, I request you to give me ordination; to get rid of suffering in order to attain enlightenment. Now I have taken these yellow robes, please ordain me with compassion. Whenever I put this robe on, I will always think about the vows that I have undertaken. I am putting away from me all that is of myself – my hair, my body, my teeth and my nails – and will think from now onward only of the path to enlightenment."

He then holds out his arms to receive a bundle of neatly-folded orange robes. He takes them to the chief monk, who puts an orange ribbon around Dias's neck and attaches it to the sash around the bundle. It is all happening so fast that one transformation runs into another. Next Dias is led away and stripped of his modern shorts and shirt. His helper wraps a long cloth around him, then puts another over his shoulder and ties a sash around his waist. Dias is now dressed in the traditional rich-orange, age-old robes of the Buddhist order. He is a monk.

Looking back later, he says: "I had no particular feeling. I was just wondering and thinking – it was all new to me."

And so the mothers leave with their own pride and sadness and the little monks go off to begin their new lives and their long working days. It is hard to recognise which of them is Dias.

Dias's mother says: "When we want to, we can go to see him. But such occasions are rare as we do not want to disturb him in his new way of life. And it would not be right to call him to our house. He is now expected to be away from us, free of family troubles, following the way of Buddha. And Dias does not reply to our letters because there is nothing to tell us about except that he is well."

TRANSFORMATION: 'It was all new to me.'

Dias remembers: "When my mother paid her respects to me, I felt uneasy and when she went away, I felt sad. But I was able to cope with it because I had already been on my own in the Galle Temple."

The boy of eleven is now in an adult world and settles down to the life he describes so calmly, sharing it with millions of other monks. His training will lead him away from childish interests and personal wants and along the spiritual path. If Dias does not settle into this world, then he can leave the monastic order and go back to being a child in a family in Sri Lanka.

But his mother says: "I am certain that he will not return. I have emphatically told him that he should stick to the robes and not leave under any circumstances. I have warned him not to return home if he leaves the robes. In fact, I have told him not to call me mother if he ever returns."

There is little chance of that, for there is a gentle conviction in Dias's voice when he says: "Till I die I will remain a monk."

LAURA: THE DOUBLE BELIEF

'God created the world and his people and animals. When it is dry, we all gather to pray for rain to the god of the mountain – Imbabura'

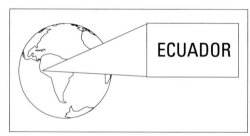

ECUADOR

LAURA knows exactly what she believes. She believes that God created the heaven and the earth and mankind. She also believes that the mountains are gods and that when people die their souls are taken to great underground rivers that link up with the overground lakes and streams.

And for Laura, a Quechan Indian, the youngest of seven in a family living high up in the remote Andean mountains of Ecuador, there is absolutely no conflict in the two ideas.

When asked about her religion Laura says she is a Catholic, a regular church-goer who attends mass with her family each week and is frequently asked to light the candles. Laura's version of the creation story could be told by almost anyone who has been to Sunday school. "Jesus God mixed earth, water and fire and in a day this world came to be," she says. "He watched and in five days he created the world. First of all he separated the water from the fire and the fire from the earth. He made the land and the lake, then he put his white clouds in place. After that he realised that everything was good and he made one woman and one man very alike to him.

"Then he placed his people and his animals in a beautiful garden. In the middle of this garden, Adam and Eve did something evil and the Father was very angry and duly threw them out of the garden. This garden and the earth had the same name."

But when Laura explains in greater detail, a very different image of the world starts to unfold. Laura's beliefs are not just based on the Bible stories she has heard in church. They are also based in a world dominated by mountains and lakes which are the homes of gods and spirits.

As Laura helps her family tilling the ground, feeding the tethered cows and repairing the straw thatch, her vision is constantly overshadowed by the great Andean peak known as Imbabura. Mount Imbabura is sacred – for Quechan Indians mountains are deities. It sits alongside another peak known as Cotacachi and is surrounded by a group of smaller mountains. Laura tells the story of the mountains as she has heard it told and retold countless times by her parents and her grandparents.

"Imbabura got married to a salt miller called Cotacachi. The miserable salt miller got pregnant and gave birth. As the child was born a whistling sound began to come out of the middle of some stones, but it stopped soon after. The child was a black mountain and was called Yanahurco. Now it sits alongside the Cotacachi mountain. When the mountain child Yanahurco was young he used to walk all over the valleys making friends and looking for a wife. Eventually he got married and had two sons. They are all mountains now."

Just below Laura's home lies the great lake of San Paulo, which has its own story.

"Many years ago a woman was working on her farm collecting food into a big pot. After a while she got tired, so she put down her pot and lay down to rest. She fell asleep and then it started to rain so much that when she woke up she found her pot was full of water. The first

BELIEF: 'Old people say the lake screams like thunder as the dead people flock back there.'

thing she did was try to throw out the water. But she couldn't because the water kept coming. The more she poured the more the water came, as if from nowhere, until this great lake was formed."

Christian and Quechan creation stories seem to sit quite comfortably side by side in Laura's mind. And when it comes to prayer the two faiths become completely intermingled. Laura is used to praying in church to the Holy Father, but sometimes her prayers are directed to a different Father, the mountain god Imbabura, especially when the crops are failing because of shortage of rain.

"Sometimes it's very dry here. Then we climb up to the foot of the mountain to ask for rain so the harvest is good enough for everybody. We all gather together and pray to the god of the mountain, Imbabura. As we pray we call him Father. We ask our Father God to give us fruit in abundance. Sometimes we come up here with our parents and celebrate mass. After we have shouted our prayers to the mountain we collect some wood to take home to make brushes in order to make our houses clean."

This curious blend of Quechan and Catholic extends to every aspect of Laura's religious life. The major Christian festivals are celebrated with everyone dressed in their best clothes, a brass band-led procession down the main street and much feasting. Such events require a lot of preparation and Laura's family are frequently at the centre of things. Take All Souls Day. Everyone helps to mix the vast bowl of bread dough that is shaped into the Quechan equivalent of gingerbread men. Once baked, baskets of bread and other offerings are taken up to the cemetery. Everyone dresses up in long woollen shirts and shawls with braided hair and beads, even for the smallest girls.

"We go up to the cemetery to pray for the souls of the dead. We take food to them because we believe souls are hungry after they die. We give the food as an offering on an altar. Everyone comes to pray – adults, old people, children. My grandmother is dead and so is my father's father. They are both buried in Otavalo. But we must feed not just our own dead relatives, but all the dead people of the community. And while we pray we give the food to them as offerings. Then we go to one side and we pray again. After we have finished praying we eat the food. I believe the dead people are in Heaven where they have followed God; they follow God when they are inside the earth."

Souls going to heaven follows Christian faith, but again when Laura explains more about what happens after death her answers become more mysterious. Laura follows the traditional Quechan belief that the souls of the dead are inside the earth. Underground is believed to be a network of flowing streams of water, rivers and lakes which connect with the lakes and rivers on the surface of the earth enabling souls to travel back and forth from the underworld of the dead. Lakes and other places where souls may surface can be dangerous to humans. Perhaps this helps explain another story that Laura tells about the lake in her own village.

"Old people have told me about the lake. They say that sometimes the lake cries and screams like thunder. They say it is the dead people who lived near the lagoons, flocking back there to wash. Sometimes they say that people who are swimming or fishing or washing clothes in the lake – they disappear. The lake takes them. It takes all the blood from those people. Then the next week the lagoon throws up their bodies again. They appear on the shore. They say you can see it all, all their bloated shapes on the shore. I've never heard the lake crying, but my grandparents have told me about it. And my father has heard a similar lagoon cry. He says the lake cries as if it's in pain."

Souls in heaven and in lakes, deities of the church and the mountains, Catholic symbolism and ritual intermingled with Quechan without any apparent contradiction – that is the mystery of Laura's belief.

FAMILY: The Quechans have always refused to lose their culture.

PRIDE OF THE QUECHAN INDIANS

LAURA'S eldest sister is one of the leaders in the community and shares with other Quechans a proud hostility to the outside world as threatening to pollute their lifestyle and corrupt their children. This is hardly surprising. Ancient Quechan civilization once ruled almost the whole of the great Andean chain through Ecuador and Peru, Bolivia and Chile. Then in the middle of the sixteenth century they were conquered by the Spanish, concentrated into small areas of land and forced into labour and Catholicism. They never fully recovered and now live in scattered communities throughout the high Andes. It takes a five-mile haul up a treacherous mountain pass to reach Laura's village. Her family are subsistence farmers who supplement their income through their handicraft skills, especially knitting, making rugs and weaving. There's always a demand for their crafts especially from tourists who visit the market places of local towns. But Laura's community have never allowed their ancient culture to become totally submerged by the lifestyle and values of modern Latin America. Laura's beliefs illustrate a continuing resistance to cultural invasion.

JACOB: THE BAR MITZVAH

'I learn to recite the text of the Torah, when to stop, when to stress words and the significance of each verse'

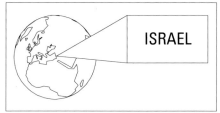

ISRAEL

BECOMING a teenager has special significance for Jacob, a Jewish boy growing up in a religious kibbutz in Israel. Once he is thirteen he is ready for his Bar Mitzvah.

Afterwards he will be accepted as a full member of the community. He will attend services at the synagogue alongside all the men on the kibbutz. In the eyes of the congregation he is ready to leave behind his childhood and take on the religious responsibilities of a man. As one of the congregation says: "This is a big event in his young life because now he is going to become a member of the congregation. And you don't do it so lightly because it is a tough job to be a member of the congregation; you have to be there on time and they count on you. And you count on them, because ten people make a congregation and if one is missing all the other nine people can't perform their religious duties. So now he's a man."

Jacob is growing up in a family which has clear rules to follow. Every day he gets up at six thirty and recites prayers with his family. After breakfast he goes to school until early afternoon.

Meanwhile his parents are busy all morning working on the chicken farm which accounts for a major part of the kibbutz's economy. His father is repsonsible for raising 35,000 broiler chickens and his mother is head of quality control in the hatchery. They come together again for lunch in the dining room along with all their other friends in the community.

Jacob's father grew up in the United States. He came with his wife to Israel in search of a close-knit community where they could bring up their family according to Jewish law and customs.

WORKER: *'I fix holes in the pipes.'*

On the kibbutz fundamental beliefs, values and lifestyles are shared among all the members and conveyed to the next generation through family life, school, work and play, as well as worship. "As a religious Jew I felt the need to be part of a community. When you're living on a religious kibbutz those laws which concern man to man, you can do them more naturally. When there are older people you take care of them because they're part of your society. If there's a celebration, the community – as a community – participates in the celebration. It is not every person by himself but every person as part of the

SACRED TEXT: 'In the Torah there are no signs, so I have to learn stresses off by heart.'

community." During the afternoon Jacob is expected to work in the kibbutz, learning a trade. He has chosen to be apprenticed as a plumber and already feels he is good enough to be entrusted to work on a small job on his own.

"I fix holes in the pipes under the ground. We put new pipes under the ground for new houses and we take parts of old pipes and we clean them by machine. Then they get put together and can be used again."

Later in the afternoon he returns home, does his homework and has free time. But in recent months he has had to forfeit some of his play time to prepare for his Bar Mitzvah. He has had special lessons, learning the sacred texts that he will have to read at the ceremony and studying Jewish law.

"I learn to recite the text, when to pause and when to stop and when to accentuate the words. In the Torah there aren't any cantillation signs, so I have to learn the stresses off by heart. I must also know the significance of each verse." As Jacob's thirteenth birthday approaches, he starts to feel nervous. He has watched his older brothers pass through their Bar Mitzvahs and has good memories of the parties that followed. But this time the spotlight is on him. All the older men will be watching with high expectations. Jacob becomes 13 on a normal working day, so the ceremony is held very early in the morning. He enters the synagogue, but at first he sits in the wrong place. He soon realises his mistake, finds the correct seat, places a black shawl, {the tallit} around his shoulders and his cap on his head. His older brother picks up a small black leather box attached to straps and begins to wind it around his arm and hand. He winds the leather thongs slowly so that Jacob can watch and copy. By now Jacob has relaxed enough to grin at his brother as they put another strap around their heads with a small box right in the centre of their foreheads. Jacob does not find this so easy.

These boxes are called phylacteries and contain small portions of the Jewish sacred text, the Torah. Jacob is now ready to stand before a big table in the centre of the Synagogue, flanked by

MAN: *Jacob's childhood is suddenly over.*

his father and two elders. Curtains at the front of the synagogue are drawn to one side revealing a recess known as The Ark. Inside is a large, heavy scroll with wooden handles adorned with silver. This is the Torah. The Law and teaching given by God to Moses on Mount Sinai is written on it by hand in black ink on parchment. As the scroll is carried to the table members of the congregation touch it with their shawls. Then it is unlocked and unrolled ceremoniously in front of Jacob. He reads the Law huskily but without faltering, then pauses and looks up shyly at the congregation who have been listening attentively. They are all men. There is only one woman in the room, dressed in black and with her head covered. Jacob's mother is not part of the congregation, but is looking down on her son from a balcony above.

Jacob continues to read the Torah in a clear voice and without stumbling. It is important that he reads well so that all in the Synagogue can hear. At this moment he is considered to be the mouthpiece of God's Word. The elder beside him then covers the Torah with a cloth and recites prayers accepting Jacob into the Jewish faith. He tells him that he is now a full member of the Jewish community and must observe the Jewish law. He must keep the Ten Commandments.

Finally Jacob's father takes the Torah and flourishes it high in the air, facing the congregation. Then Jacob rolls it up, bringing both scroll handles into the centre ready for its return to The Ark. The final words that Jacob hears are: "The Lord bless thee and keep thee." The ceremony is over and with it Jacob's official childhood. Suddenly, following a tradition more than three thousand years old, he is a man. He is now fully a Jew.

BARBARA: FIRST COMMUNION

'I am very pleased that I shall receive communion. It means that God has selected me to serve and love Him'

ZIMBABWE

MY NAME is Barbara and I live in Gwindi village in Zimbabwe. I am twelve years old. There are eight of us in our family, all of us girls. Plus our parents. I give my parents my love, and so I help them. I herd cattle, fetch water from the well, guard the garden to prevent cattle getting in, clean the house and sometimes I do the cooking.

But today is a special day for me because I am going to receive my first Communion. That means that I shall receive the flesh and blood of Christ. Then I won't be alone any more because Jesus Christ will be with me. My mother says that the Catholic Church is the only one which God originally established, and so it is the true church. I am very pleased that I shall receive my first Communion. It means that God has selected me to serve and love Him and therefore God has chosen me to be with Him. I am expected

FAITH: 'When I confess my sins, God forgives.'

to obey God's commandments and carry out God's work – for example by giving help to those in need and by caring for others who may not be able to take care of themselves.

Jesus said: "You should carry on my work." So that's what I'm going to do. I will do all the duties required of me as a Christian, such as helping others, being prepared to have patience and listen, lessening the burden on others who may be in difficulties by offering to help. I am preparing myself by observing and obeying the Ten Commandments, such as not stealing or lying, and by not provoking others for no apparent reason, by forgiving those that have done us some harm or wronged us. I know that when I confess all my sins, the Lord God will forgive me, for God has mercy and loves all of us.

So, when I receive the body and blood of Christ I am expected to obey God's commandments, to do my best to carry out God's work. That's why today is a special day for me.

UMAR: FASTING FOR RAMADAN

'We're supposed to be obedient, not fight or swear and things like that, and we don't eat until it's sunset'

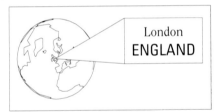

London
ENGLAND

HIGH UP in a block of flats within sight and sound of Big Ben, Umar explains why he has had nothing to eat since dawn.

"We fast in the month of Ramadan. It was the prophet Mohammed, peace be upon him, who made the rules. They're in the Koran. We're supposed to be obedient, not fight, swear and things like that, cos it's a month when you're supposed to be religious. Each day we don't break our fast until it's sunset. Then we can eat. This year it has been hard because the summer days are long."

LEARNING: 'English is easier.'

Umar's family are Palestinian, but they live in the heart of London. During the month of Ramadan, only Umar's four-year-old sister Aishah is excused from fasting, for the time being at least.

"The Koran says that a good Muslim must pray five times each day. The first prayer is Fajr. That's at about 4-4.30 in the morning. We get up for that, all except my sister Aishah. She stays asleep. It's too early for her. The next prayer is Duhr. We do that at my school at about one o'clock. The third prayer is called Asr. I do it straight away when I get home from school at about five o'clock. The fourth prayer we do at sunset, which is about 8.30. That's the Maghrib. Then the last prayer we do is the Isha, that's at about 9.30 or maybe 10."

So by the time Big Ben strikes four Umar has already been woken up for a very early breakfast. After a few more hours in bed he sets off for the King Fahad Academy in Acton. The school gives a lot of attention to Arabic, Islamic religion and prayers, including the elaborate washing rituals.

"Before we pray we do our ablution. First we do our hands three times, then we do our mouth three times, and our nose three times and our face three times, both our arms three times and our hair once and ears once and our feet, both feet, three times. This is important so that when we're praying we're nice and fresh."

In other respects Umar's school-days are not so different from other London children's, except when it comes to lunchtime. For throughout Ramadan there is no lunch. The boys go out to play but the chairs in the dining hall remain stacked on top of the tables.

Meanwhile little Aishah is attending a pre-school group at the Muslim centre where she is already learning to recite short passages from the Koran. She is quite keen to start fasting with the rest of the family, but her mother will not let her for a few years yet. "You have to train the

DEVOUT: 'The Koran says that a good Muslim must pray five times each day.'

children to fast," she explains. "I started Umar when he was about eight. In the first year I let him do half a day and then a full day and then a week. In the second year two weeks, and so on, gradually breaking him in. Now that he's eleven, he's ready to fast the whole month."

During the journey back from school Umar does his best to ignore the tantalising displays in food shops and cafes and the snack Aishah gets while they are watching TV at home. Umar was born in England, but he thinks of Palestine as his homeland and follows news of the conflict there. The family often talk in Arabic, but Umar feels more at home in English.

"My dad talks Arabic the most. My mother sometimes talks Arabic, sometimes English. Me and my brother and sister mostly talk English. It's easier to talk English because I've been living here all my life. It's the same with writing. English is quite easy to learn when you're little. When you're big, learning Arabic is quite hard. I can read Arabic all right, but it's the spelling that's the hardest thing."

When Umar comes down from the flats to run an errand for his mother, he is aware of the slowly-lengthening shadows that mean he will not have to wait too much longer for food. But he accepts the discipline without complaint. As always, prayers come first. With daylight fading the family make their preparations. Each of them knows their place.

"First we lay out a mat to face Mecca. Then my dad stands in the front row because he's the Imam. Me and my brother stand in the second row and my mum and my sister stand in the third row."

It is more than fifteen hours since breakfast. Evening prayers over, the lights of London's nightlife begin to come on and Umar's family sit down for the meal of the day. As the month wears on the days grow longer and dinnertime gets later. Umar can always tell you to the minute what time sunset is that day. He is also very aware of the moon.

"When we see the full moon on the 29th or 30th day we finish fasting and have our Eid prayers. Lots of us go to a special place in the park to pray. The Imam gives a lecture, then we go back to the mosque to eat, have games, win prizes, all that stuff. It's a bit like Christmas."

CHAPTER NINE: FAREWELL TO CHILDHOOD

CATHY & JAMES:MOVING ON

'You have to have a uniform, not just any old clothes. I wanted a white shirt, but my mum said white wouldn't wash as well as grey, knowing me'

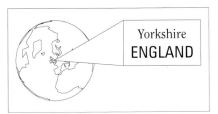

Yorkshire
ENGLAND

FOR every baby born into the six communities in Chapter One, there is another child about to leave childhood behind. We return to these communities now to meet girls and boys as they make the transition into adolescence.

CATHY and JAMES both live just across the village green from baby Jenny's house in the heart of the Yorkshire Dales. It was James who came to Simeon's rescue on his first day at the tiny village school {see Page 93}. Now it is James's turn to be one of the new boys in the very different atmosphere of a secondary school.

JAMES: Next term we are going to start secondary school. So last week we went to buy our uniform. You have to have a uniform for that school. You can't just go in any old clothes. We got jumpers and lots of things like that, but it were so hot.

CATHY: There were PE skirts and knickers, orange socks, T-shirts, shirts, tie, grey socks. In the skirts there were pleats and cuts and all kinds of things. When I tried all the things on I looked like a beanstalk, an overgrown beanstalk. And James looked the same I think, a beanstalk.

JAMES: I tried about three pairs of trousers on before we eventually got the right size. Then we had to get my swimming trunks. We tried the first pair on and they nearly crippled me, and then we tried another on and they weren't much better and then we tried another pair and they fit. Next we got some shorts for inside and some shorts for outside for playing rugby, and a rugby top and socks. Last I got a grey shirt. I wanted a white shirt but my mum said a white shirt wouldn't wash as well as grey, knowing me.

CATHY: Right now I can be at school in two minutes, but when I start secondary school I'll have to take the bus that goes around all the up-dale villages before it gets to school. It takes an hour each way. I'm quite looking forward to being in a new class and the gym.

JAMES: I'm looking forward to the woodwork and there being more boys in the class. And I'm looking forward to the athletics side, the running, rugby, cricket and swimming. All stuff like that.

CHANGE: 'It will take an hour to get there.'   *SKILL: 'I'm looking forward to woodwork.'*

XIAO FUNG:MIDDLE LEADER

'When I was little I enjoyed playing games with my friends, but now I don't any more. I want to be a mathematician and read more books'

Xi'an
CHINA

LI XIAO FUNG lives just down the road from Jin Jin's house in the central Chinese industrial town of Xi'an. She is still in the final year of primary school, but already has clear ambitions.

'At school I'm a middle leader. A middle leader's major responsibility is for class discipline, among other things. In my class I lead the morning reading session, morning exercises and so on. We also have a senior leader in our class. He mainly gives us information and delegates various responsibilities. We also have a representative on the school's cultural and recreational team, which organises cultural events and we have a representative on the hygiene committee. There are other junior leaders who are responsible for giving out and collecting exercise books.

During our spare time, my sisters and I normally stay at home and read. We are very interested in science, so we enjoy reading scientific magazines. I like being with my sisters because if there is anything I don't understand I can always ask them. But if they don't know the answers I try to look them up in reference books .

When I was little I enjoyed playing games with my friends. We used to play 'elastics' – jumping over a line made of elastic bands, or throwing little sacks made of sand. Also we used to collect apricot stones to play the game of 'Jacks'. But now I'm a lot older I don't play those kinds of games any more.

Every Wednesday afternoon when there is no school, I go to the park with my schoolfriends – there's me, the class junior leader and our team leaders. We hold a meeting where we have to think about certain topics. I remember once the theme of the meeting was 'Imaginary Inventions'. That was very interesting. One of our class-mates came up with the idea of creating a very special jacket – one that you could wear all the year round. The inside of the jacket would be made up of special cells that would swell in the winter, making people feel very warm, but shrink back to their normal size in the summer, making the jacket feel very cool and comfortable to wear.

I want to be a mathematician in the future. I want to spend my spare time reading more books on mathematics, so that I can do more for the human race. Since ancient times, China has been important for mathematics, and I would like to explore that too. I would really like to go to university, but I'm not confident about getting in. I have read in the newspaper that people can't afford to pay the fees, so not enough are going there. I don't think it's absolutely necessary for mathematicians to go to university. If they have learned about university-level mathematics in their spare time and also during their middle and high school careers, their intellectual ability should be higher than that of university graduates.'

AIMS: 'I would like to explore mathematics so that I can do more for the human race.'

DANIEL: BECOMING A MAN

'All the other boys my age will be circumcised, so it's OK. I won't feel anything until I'm back home again. And then I will be a young man'

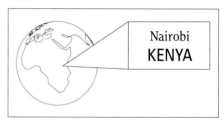

Nairobi
KENYA

IN THE Kikuyu Highlands of Kenya, not far from the tiny plot of land where Hannah plays among the maize, thirteen-year-old Daniel must prepare for a ritual initiation into manhood.

'I already feel quite quite grown up, but before I am accepted as an adult I must first be circumcised. I believe it is good because there's an age you need to reach before you undergo the initiation ceremony. It's normal for boys to be circumcised before they go to secondary school.

I like going to school. I'm in class 7, with one more class to go before I go on to secondary school, as long as my father can get enough money to pay for the books and clothes. My teacher is pleased with my work. I have been learning English for about five years. It's good to learn English because I may go somewhere where people don't speak Kikuyu and I will need to be able to speak English. I like playing football and I'm the captain and centre-forward in the school team. We don't have boots, so we have to wear what we have, so many of us play barefoot. That's OK as long as the ball isn't blown up too hard. Then it hurts.

My father is often out with the donkeys collecting 'munyu' from the rocks. He sells it to people to give to their cattle and goats *{as a mineral supplement}*. My mother left home five years ago because she had so many arguments with my father. He didn't agree with the church she went to. He told her to stop going there but she refused so he made her leave. She took my little sisters with her and just left me with my brothers and my father. We were left with all the work that she used to do at home.

So while he's away I'm the oldest boy left at home. I'm expected to do a lot of the jobs and look after my younger brothers, Joseph and David. We taught ourselves how to cook and wash the dishes. We have to take the animals out to the fields and cultivate crops on our land. My father keeps many animals and grows many crops such as potatoes, maize, pumpkins, cassava. We also have to sweep and fetch water. But the biggest job is getting firewood. The nearest good place is nearly seven miles away. We have to take a donkey cart to carry it home, or bring it on our backs. We pass other trees on the way, but we aren't allowed to cut them because they are 'mugha' *{acacia trees}*, planted to stop the soil getting blown away. Such trees are no good for burning, so we walk on. It takes all day to collect enough firewood for cooking for just one week.

I have one other job at home – making ropes out of the sisal leaves that grow nearby. I have to strip off the soft parts of the leaves and plait the fibres to make them strong. I learned about ropes when I was a small boy by watching older men at work. At first my ropes were no good, but now we use them to tie up the donkeys, carry the wood and lift the water buckets. When I've finished at school, I would like to get a special kind of job, like a doctor or a car mechanic repairing cars, or planes, or anything like that. I have seen the inside beauty of a car, and learned many names for the different parts.

My father has explained how I must begin to behave like a grown-up and not like a child. I must stop using bad language. I must stop playing with the other children and begin to take responsibility for younger boys and girls, advising and directing them. I used to fool around a lot with the other children but I won't be able to do that any more.

In the old days people used to be cut at home or at the barber's, but now the circumcision is usually done by the doctor at the clinic. I'm not afraid of going to the clinic because I've been told that I won't feel anything until I'm back home again. And all the other boys my age will be circumcised, so it's OK.

After the ceremony I have to remain in seclusion for seven days. I will stay in my older brother's hut, which is also in our compound. Once it is all over I will no longer be a child. I will be a young man.

MANHOOD: 'I must behave like a grown up.'

BINDU: LEARNING A TRADE

'My parents asked me to stop school. They said I needn't go because I was ill. I want to become a tailor now and I like tailoring very much'

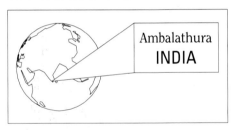

Ambalathura
INDIA

ON THE southern shores of India, much of Bindu's childhood has been spent helping to look after her two young nieces, Savitha and Kochumol. Now she has already left school to start learning a trade that will help support her large family.

'I've just left the village school after three years. I had been ill for a while and when I went back they'd struck my name off the register and said I couldn't be re-admitted. But in any case I'd decided I was too old and wanted to leave. My parents asked me to stop. They said I needn't go because I was ill. I want to become a tailor and now my Aunty Indira is teaching me. I like tailoring very much. First I learnt to stitch shorts and panties. Now I can stitch a skirt and a blouse and a petticoat. My Aunty Indira cuts out for me, but I will have to learn cutting now. People bring the material to be stitched to our home. I will take it and give it to Aunty Indira and she will take the sample blouse and take the measurement and cut it. It takes about an hour to cut. Then we will stitch it and deliver it and I will collect the money and give it to Aunty Indira. I also help my family with their work. My grandfather and my mother wash clothes. So do my father, my uncle and my brothers. I fetch water for washing the clothes. When they're dry and ironed, I deliver them back and collect the money.

Now that my sister Usha lives away at Chandran's house, I look after Kochumol a lot. I play with her and the other children. Sometimes I make the food for my family. I fetch wood to light the fire and then set a pot of water on it. Then I wash the rice and set it on to cook. At the end I sieve it. If I am cooking fish, I grind chilli, coriander and turmeric to make a curry. Other times I make vegetable curries. Then I use coconut. Sometimes I have to go to the market to buy the food. But my parents don't allow me to go to far-off places on my own. I don't go to visit friends' houses. I meet them on the road and then we talk. But they don't visit me and I don't visit them.

I play games with Kochumol and Savitha. I tell them to make rice and curry. We pick green leaves and grind them. We take sand and pretend that it's rice. Then I go away to stitch and they play on their own.

I don't know how many years it will be until I get married. But the kind of person I would want to marry must not be the type who runs after other women. He should not drink arrack, I don't like a person who drinks. He should work hard and look after my parents and provide for me. He does not have to be too good-looking. He will be a person my parents find for me. My only wish in life is for my parents to live a long life. Other than that, I have no wish.'

CARING: 'I look after my niece. The man I marry won't run after other women or drink.'

ZOLTAN: THE RAILWAYMAN

'The hardest job is being the controller because if you misread the time and let a train go, that could cause a crash'

Budapest
HUNGARY

IN THE same Hungarian city where Szabolcs is growing up, Zoltan is still at school. But he is getting experience of adult working lives by helping to run the Pioneer Railway. He is learning responsibility and being part of a team.

'MY NAME is Zoltan. I work on the Pioneer Railway in Budapest. Here everything is done by the children themselves. There are only two adults – the engine-driver and the station-master. They supervise us. They make sure we do everything right. I shout out things like: "Can I see your tickets please? The next station is Sagvari-liget."

My mother used to be a pioneer railwayman and my sister is one too. So when school said I could apply for a course I was keen to do it. You have to have good school results to be allowed. And your eyes have to be good. You have to be able to see colours well.

We had to do a lot of classes and then take an exam. I was asked about signalling, shifting points, how to send messages from one station to another, how to control the movement of the trains, and about safety devices. Then there are all the things to do with tickets: the prices; who gets free passes; how to sell, check and collect them; the work of the inspector, and so on. The other thing about the railway is that we carry the mail. So we have to learn all about postal rates and that sort of thing.

I passed, and then there was a big graduation ceremony. I liked that very much. There were nearly 150 of us all lined up in our uniforms. We were in our summer uniform, which is blue. But in the winter we wear a grey outfit with a long warm coat and a cap, of course. We saluted the flag, sang the national anthem and then took the oath. It went:

'I, Zoltan, a young member of the Pioneer Railway, swear in front of the flag and the other Pioneers that I will observe the rules of Pioneer life, the regulations of the railway under all circumstances. I will preserve the good reputation of the Pioneer Railway. I will serve my socialist country and the working people with my acts.'

The only problem with the ceremony was that I had to stand there for such a long time.

I started work on the railway straight after that. We work in teams. There are fifteen complete teams, so my turn only comes up once every fifteen days. Those days I have to miss school. I get up really early, like at 5.45, and get a tram down to the railway.

They give us breakfast, then we're taken up to one of the stations to start work, or we're assigned to one of the trains, or other jobs. We don't finish until six in the evening, and then we have group work until seven, before we're allowed to go home. Most of all I like doing the job

TICKETS PLEASE: 'The railway is great. It's teaching me to think and it's good fun.'

of cashier, looking after all the money. After that I like being an announcer, using the public address system. The most difficult job is being the controller, because if you misread the time and let a train go at the wrong time that could cause the trains to crash, and people might get injured. That wouldn't be good at all.

I think the railway is great. I don't know what I would do without it. I never get bored. There isn't time, because we are the ones that have to do everything. The Pioneer Railway is teaching me how to think for myself. I've been learning what I can do in the world, how I can be useful. And it's good fun.

FABIANA: A FIRST BOYFRIEND

'Pedro's fifteen. I feel I'm good for him and he's good for me, but I'm going out with him secretly. I don't think my parents would approve'

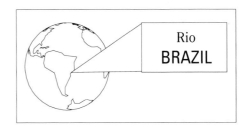

IN RIO de Janeiro's Santa Marta favela, Fabiana has long been responsible for much of the daily care of her little sister Marianna, especially as her mother works long hours. She has already stopped playing childish games with her friends when she has free time. Instead, she prefers to 'go out' whenever she can. And as a final farewell to childhood – even though she would still prefer her parents not to know – she has a boyfriend.

'MY NAME is Fabiana. I'm 12 years old and I live on the hillsides above Rio de Janeiro. I'm still at school, but I don't find it easy. So the teachers make me stay in second grade. A lot of my friends have already left school.They kept missing lessons, so the teacher cut them off the register. So now they sit around at home and do nothing.

I still go to school in the mornings. And when I'm not in school I help my mother a lot at home. I spend a lot of time looking after Marianna and Angelica – they're my smallest sisters. Before I go to school, I get them up, dress them, give them their breakfast and play with them. When I get back from school I often do washing and ironing. I give the little ones their baths and make them their dinner too. That's the thing I like most – making food. The thing I like least is cleaning the toilet.

When I'm not working at home what I most like doing is going out. Whenever I can I go out with my friends. We go out walking, down the hill to the park. Sometimes we go down to the beach. That's our favourite place. But my father restricts what I can do. He always tells me what time I've got to get back. If I go out out at four o'clock he says I've got to get back home by six o'clock sharp. So I arrive at six sharp. Then he doesn't even give me time to have some fun. It seems that I'm a nun.

I want to get married when I'm eighteen. I'd like to marry a man who isn't an alcoholic. I want him to be a good, content, happy person – rich or poor it doesn't matter. I don't want him to be rough like the husbands of other women are, I'd like him to be gentle-hearted. I'd like to live in an apartment and have two children, a boy and a girl. Just the two of them. I don't want seven or eight children like my mum, because they make too much work.

I do have a boyfriend already – most of the girls in my school do. My boyfriend is called Pedro. He's fifteen. I feel I'm good for him and he's good for me. I met him here in the favela – but I'm going out with him secretly. We don't go very far away. We stay close to home. But my parents don't know anything about him. I don't think they would approve.'

FAMILY PLANS: 'I want two children, not seven or eight like my mum. Too much work.'